Discovery
and
Renewal
on
Huffman Prairie

Discovery and Renewal on
Huffman

The Kent State University Press ⟨⟩ Kent, Ohio

Prairie

Where Aviation Took Wing

David Nolin

Frontis: Quilt depicting Huffman Prairie State Natural Landmark by Diane Dover.

All unattributed photos or figures are by the author.

Contents

. . . .

Foreword

When most people think of the Wright brothers and the invention of the airplane, Kitty Hawk comes to mind. Each year, millions of Americans visit the great national memorial that marks the spot where the two brothers from Dayton, Ohio, first took to the sky in powered flight. But the invention of the airplane was not the work of a single morning. The Wrights had laid the foundation for success with experiments involving an evolutionary series or aircraft—one kite (1899), three gliders (1900, 1901, 1902), and a few weeks of critically important tests with a homemade wind tunnel. With the four short flights of December 17, 1903, under their belts, the brothers built on their initial success by continuing their experiments at Huffman Prairie, just eight miles east of their home in Dayton.

In this little remnant of the great prairies that had once spread across Ohio, Wilbur and Orville Wright would continue their work, attracting little notice as they built and flew two more powered aircraft in 1904 and 1905, gaining experience in the air and fine-tuning their design. On October 5, 1905, Wilbur Wright circled over Huffman Prairie, flying 24 miles (38.9 km) in 39 minutes, 23 seconds. The airplane became a practical reality in the sky over an Ohio pasture, which would continue as the Wrights established their flying school on the prairie in 1910, followed by the Army Air Service, which began using the land in 1917. Today the field where it all began is a part of the giant research and development complex that is Wright-Patterson Air Force Base.

But Huffman Prairie had been a place of discovery long before the Wright brothers arrived on the scene. Beginning in the 1830s, botanists identified new prairie plant species in this prairie. In the decades that followed, the area remained a favorite botanical hunting ground. Its unique natural character was forgotten, however, as government fences went up and eyes turned to the sky. In a remarkable sense, that the government acquired this field at such an early date has helped to preserve an idea of what occurred here. The modern Wright Brothers National Memorial, standing where the Wrights first flew, is a commemorative environment, quite unlike the sandy beach that the inventors of the airplane knew. Standing alone on Huffman Prairie on a quiet summer afternoon, your back to the main base runway, looking west toward Wright Hill; however, it could almost be 1905. Like the local farmers at the beginning of the twentieth century, you can almost hear the rattle and pop of the engine as Wilbur and Orville prepare for another flight.

Dave Nolin, the author of the book you hold in your hands, is largely responsible for the renaissance of interest in Huffman Prairie as a great natural treasure. Since his time as a graduate student at Wright State University, he has worked tirelessly to study the prairie, restore it to something of its glory, and find new ways to share this little piece of the original Ohio landscape with the rest of us. You could not ask for a better guide to the geological, natural, and human history of this little patch of the original Ohio landscape.

Tom D. Crouch
Senior Curator, Aeronautics
National Air and Space Museum
Smithsonian Institution

Acknowledgments

Many people have provided much-needed editorial help, great advice, and access to a wealth of information, which made this book possible.

I would like to thank Tom Crouch for his encouragement and advice over the years, for reviewing the manuscript, and for his kind foreword. Thanks also to Jim Amon, Guy Denny, Paul Knoop, Jim McCormac, Jacob Nolin, Bob Petersen, Ryan Qualls, Carrie Scarff, Ann Snively, and Kathleen Walters for reviewing the manuscript. I am very grateful to Trudy Krisher for publishing advice. The book's historical elements were possible only with the assistance of the Wright State University Libraries Special Collections and Archives, the Greene County Archives (thanks go to Robin Heise, Joan Donovan, and Elise Kelly), the Greene County Recorder's Office (Eric Sears and Tammy Cox), the Greene County Room at the Greene County Public Library, the Dayton Metro Library Genealogy Center (Jamie McQuinn), the Miami Conservancy District (Deborah Janning), the Archives/Library of the Ohio History Connection in Columbus, the Boonshoft Museum of Discovery (Lynn Hanson), and Bath Township (Elaine Brown). I obtained historical information on Wright Patterson Air Force Base with the help of Base Historian Henry Narducci, and Cultural Resources Manager Paul Woodward. Thanks to Tony Huffman for letting me review the Huffman family historical documents.

I am very grateful to Ann Armstrong-Ingoldsby, Marge Bicknell, Liz Cramer, Robert Dafford, Dayton History, Diane Dover, Dan Enders, Roger Garber, Ann Geise, Dottie Gheen, Tom Hissong, Bob Jurick, the Library of Congress, Rick Luehrs, Jim McCormac, the Miami Conservancy District, Elisabeth Rothschild, Loraine Tai, Wright-Patterson Air Force Base,

Wright State University Archives and Special Collections, and Chong Zhang for permitting me to use their photographs and artwork.

Many have helped protect and restore the Huffman Prairie State Natural Landmark over the years. An incomplete list includes Fred Bartenstein, Karen Beason, Becky Benná, Irv Bieser, Dan Boone, Elizabeth Burke, Liz Cramer, Ron Cramer, Carol Culbertson, Jeff Davis, Guy Denny, Grace Dietsch, Mark Dillon, David Duell, Mike Enright, Woody Ensor, Jan Ferguson, Jennifer Finfera, Charles Fox, Roger Garber, Rick Gardner, Steve Goodwin, Jim Hill, Jennifer Hillmer, Mary Huffman, Debbie Karr, Kevin Kepler, Jane Klein, Paul Knoop, Marlene Kromer, Charity Krueger, Terry Lavy, Leisa Ling, Charlotte Mathena, Debby McKee, James McKee, Eric Metzler, Dave Minney, Brittney Mitchell, Dick Mosley, Dane Mutter, Greg Nash, Marvin Olinsky, William Orellana, Bob Petersen, Ralph Ramey, John Ritzenthaler, Jim Runkle, Terry Seidel, Alex Shartle, Charlie Shoemaker, Larry Smith, Pete Smith, Joe Sommers, Connie Strobbie, Danielle Trevino, Lily True, Lois Walker, current WPAFB Natural Resources Manager Darryn Warner, Jan Williams, Roger Zebold, and any others whom I don't know about or have neglected to mention.

Finally, special thanks go to retired base natural resources manager Terri Lucas for her successful efforts to have the prairie dedicated as a state natural landmark and for making the prairie a conservation focus for Wright-Patterson; Mary Klunk, whose skill and experience in prairie restoration has greatly benefitted the site; my wife, Catherine Queener, for all her love and support through the course of this project; and my father, Gervais R. Nolin, who passed in 2009 (thanks for being such a great dad, and for getting us past the security gate!).

Introduction

In 1903, Dayton, Ohio's Wright brothers flew the world's first powered aircraft on the dunes of Kitty Hawk in North Carolina. On its best flight, their 1903 Flyer managed a fifty-nine–second straight-line flight. For the next year's experiments, wanting a place closer to home, they picked a field eight miles east of Dayton, Ohio, locally known as Huffman Prairie. Here, on an eighty-four–acre pasture, in 1904 and 1905 they improved the performance of their invention and taught themselves how to control it. On a single flight on October 5, 1905, Wilbur, piloting their 1905 Flyer, the first practical airplane, circled the field nearly thirty times and stayed aloft for over thirty-nine minutes, the time it took to run the fuel tank dry.[1]

The pasture the Wright brothers used was a small piece of what had been a three-square-mile natural prairie along the Mad River in Greene County, Ohio. A prairie is a grassland found in central North America containing a diverse mix of tall grasses and flowering plants and few or no trees. Before Ohio became a state in 1803, the Mad River Valley in southwestern Ohio contained many natural prairie grasslands. These occurred as scattered patches ranging in size from less than an acre to over eight square miles and in varieties that differed depending on soil moisture levels. Each variety had its own diversity of plant and animal life, but by the mid-1900s nearly all these prairies had been drained, plowed, and converted to agricultural production.

The prairie remnant adjacent to the Wright brothers' old flying field has been of great interest to me since I first saw it in 1984. The slow unravelling of its history and the slow but steady restoration of its native diversity have been joyful learning experiences. Since I retired in August

2015, my historical research has intensified, as has my study of the site's natural history. I actually have the time to observe the habits, populations, and interactions of the prairie's plant and animal residents. I can pass long mornings in this green, open, life-filled grassland without seeing another soul. The quiet can suddenly be broken by the amazing acceleration of a modern jet fighter taking off, a visiting World War II bomber coming in, or even a replica of the Wright-B Flyer flying over the Wright brothers' old field. When the sound of the aircraft fades, the subtler sounds of birds and insects return as they go about their business among the tall grasses and flowers. A lot of people have worked to restore this piece of original Ohio prairie. Some efforts failed, some succeeded, but much has been learned over thirty-some years of work. Restoration ecology is still a new science, probably about where aviation science was in the Wright brothers' day. Knowing these things, a visit to Huffman Prairie always inspires wonder at what human beings have learned and accomplished on this open field over the last 180 years. There is still plenty more to learn.

The first five chapters of this book tell the story of how Huffman Prairie came to be, how it affected the development of aviation and the Dayton region, and how it was mostly destroyed. The last two cover the more recent history, in which I have been personally involved.

CHAPTER ONE

A Grid on the Land

In November 1803, Colonel Israel Ludlow and his seven-man team had broken camp and started another long day of surveying. They started on the west line of Section 31 in Township 3, Range 8, between the Great and Little Miami Rivers. As usual, the hunter took the lead position to procure game to feed the team before the team arrived at the next night's campsite and to keep a lookout for hostile Indians. Two chain men handled the Gunter's chain, sixty-six feet long and composed of one hundred brass links; they would lay the chain down eighty times to measure one mile, guided by Ludlow's sightings, using his tripod-mounted compass. The survey team divided the land into a grid of square-mile sections. The marker would record the team's observations and measurements. Another man, following Ludlow, handled the packhorse that carried the team's equipment and gear. The seventh team member, the spy, trailed behind about two hundred yards and made sure no one was following them.[1]

The team started in a forest of oak and hickory trees, but at eight and one-half chains it came to a small prairie. The men had encountered many of these open grasslands in the Mad River Valley. Some were dry, and some were wet, or "boggy." This prairie outlier became forest again after three chains, but after another nine the forest gave way to a large prairie that extended far to the east and west. Here, Ludlow took out his hatchet and cut a blaze on a hickory tree twenty-two inches in diameter. The team pushed through the tall grasses and marked off twenty more chains, arriving at the halfway point of the section line. There were no trees to blaze, so Ludlow picked out one of the wooden survey stakes stowed on the packhorse and pounded it into the black soil. They

Early survey crew laying chain across a prairie. Detail of *Paducah Wall to Wall, Paducah's History on Floodwall Murals*, by Dafford Muralists, artist Robert Dafford. Used with permission.

continued north through the prairie and entered a patch of young forest full of "brush, grapevines, and briars." After three more chains, they entered the prairie again and pushed through the thick grass for another twenty-four chains, where they reached the end of the section line. There were still no trees, so another post was pounded in. Ludlow summarized the nature of the land found along the newly surveyed mile, and the marker recorded, "Set a temporary post—this mile over level land—principally over prairie, much grass in said prairie." As Ludlow and the team laid out section line after section line, the outline of the more-than-two-thousand–acre prairie began to take shape on the new survey map. From south to north, the prairie stretched almost exactly three miles. On the south end, it was nearly two miles wide, but it narrowed considerably on the north end. Much of the western and southern sections of the prairie were described as "boggy prairie land" and "wet boggy prairie," while the eastern and northern sections were labeled "good prairie land" or "dry prairie."[2] Like many of the other Mad River Valley prairies, this one was bordered in part by young oak forests with thick understories of shrubs, such as wild plum and American hazelnut. These oak-hazel thickets gave way to mature oak and hickory forests.

Ludlow and his team were the action end of a large enterprise that started in the U.S. Continental Congress with the Land Ordinance of 1785. This ordinance set up a system that allowed citizens to purchase land from the undeveloped wilderness of what is now Ohio to provide compensation to Revolutionary War veterans and encourage organized settlement. The ordinance created the public land survey system to lay out rectangular grids called townships on the land, each containing thirty-six square miles.[3] The main reference points available to the surveyors were the trees of the forests that blanketed most of the land-scape. These forests were sprinkled with prairies, thickets, and wetlands, which could also be valuable reference points. To mark section corners

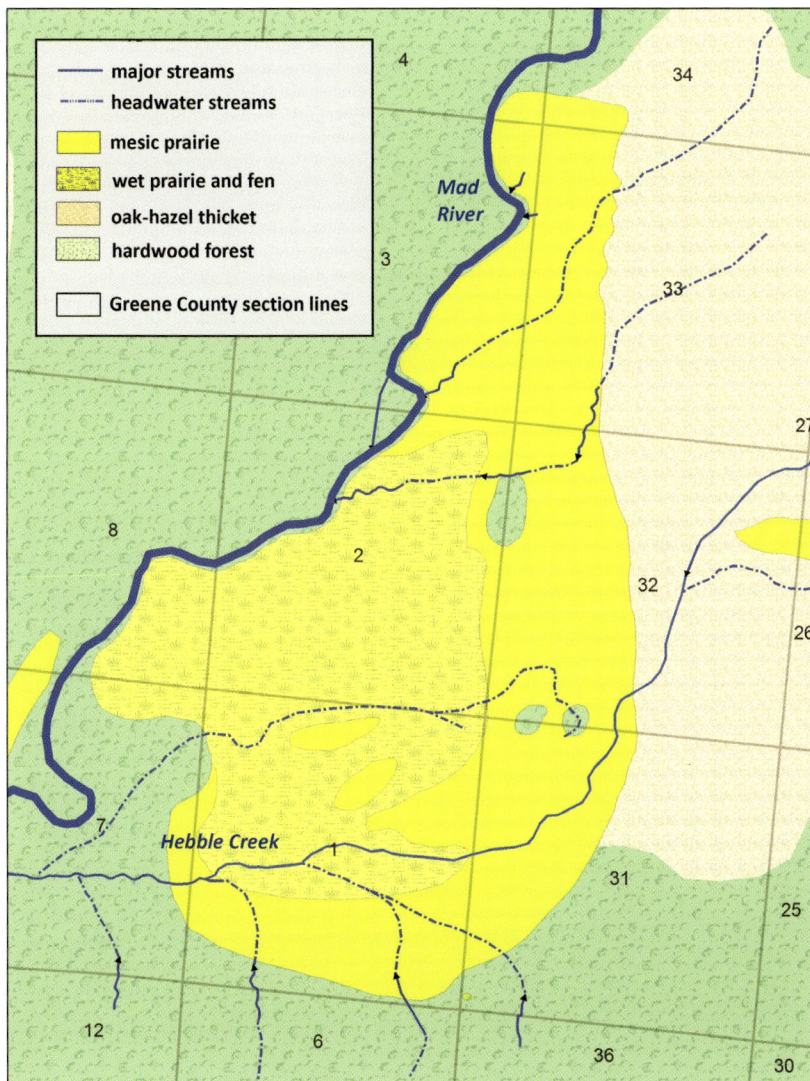

Legend:
- major streams
- headwater streams
- mesic prairie
- wet prairie and fen
- oak-hazel thicket
- hardwood forest
- Greene County section lines

Mad River

Hebble Creek

Presettlement plant communities and streams near Huffman Prairie in Bath Township, Greene County, Ohio, based on analysis of public land surveys conducted in 1802 and 1803.

Figure A

Townships within the Between the Miamis survey. Image courtesy of USGenWeb Archives.

or other notable points on a line, the surveyor used a hatchet to cut the bark from two noteworthy trees nearby. He listed the distance and bearing from the corner or point to each tree and recorded the species and diameter of the trees. Thus, the surveyors had to be able to identify the many tree species native to the Ohio Valley, in summer or winter. It also meant that the Ordinance of 1785 created not only a system to settle the wilderness but one that inadvertently made good records of the forests and vegetation that covered the land before it was settled and changed.[4]

Israel Ludlow was born in 1765 near Morristown, New Jersey.[5] In 1787, the surveyor general of the United States, Thomas Hutchins, recruited him to survey the outer boundary of a tract of land known as the Miami Purchase, Land Between the Miamis, or Symmes Purchase.[6] John Cleves Symmes, a member of the Continental Congress from New Jersey, had given considerably of his own resources to help the Continental Army during the Revolutionary War. In return for his war efforts, Congress agreed to sell him up to a million acres of land between the Great and Little Miami Rivers, but not before the land was properly surveyed.[7]

In 1788, soon after arriving in the Ohio country, Ludlow became part of a separate adventure; he partnered with two others to purchase eight hundred acres of land from Symmes, north of the Ohio River, across from the mouth of the Licking River.[8] Here, the trio laid out a new settlement, which became Cincinnati. In November 1790, Ludlow began the survey of the boundaries of the Symmes Purchase. There were many delays, caused by lack of military escorts and danger from Native Americans, all of which he described in a letter enclosed with the partially completed survey he sent to Secretary of the Treasury Alexander Hamilton in May 1792.

Philadelphia, May 5, 1792

. . . On my arrival at Fort Washington, I again applied for protection to proceed in the Miami survey. That assistance was refused by Maj. Zeigler, who then commanded (his letter I will produce). My reputation as well as the public good, being in some measure affected by the delay of the business, I was constrained to have recourse to an effort which my instruction did advise, viz.: to attempt making the survey by the aid of three active woodsmen, to assist as spies, and give notice of any approaching danger. My attempts proved unsuccessful. After extending the western boundary more than one hundred miles up the Miami River, the deep snows and cold weather rendered our situation too distressing, by reason of my men having their feet frozen, and unfit to furnish game for supplies. In consequence, we returned to Fort Washington. The cold weather abating, I made another attempt, extending the east boundary as far as the line intersected the Little Miami River, where we discovered signs of the near approach of Indians, and, having but three armed men in company, induced me to return again to Fort Washington, which I found commanded by Gen. Wilkinson, whom I applied for an escort, which was denied me (his letter I have the honor to inclose to you with the others).

I now have the satisfaction to present you the whole of the survey of the Ohio, and part of the Miami, purchases, executed agreeably to instructions. Any further information that may be required respecting the causes of delay of the above business, I presume may be had from Gens. St. Clair and Harmar, who are now here present.

I am, sir, yours respectfully

Israel Ludlow.[9]

Ludlow continued his short but remarkable career, laying out the towns of Hamilton in 1794 and Dayton in 1795.[10] Traveling north to Philadelphia in the spring of 1796, he stopped at the residence of General James Chambers, in Chambersburg, Pennsylvania. Chambers's daughter, Charlotte, immediately became enamored of Ludlow and later wrote that she considered him "the perfection of manly loveliness." They married on November 11, 1796. This meant Charlotte had to relocate to Cincinnati and undertake a long journey through the wilderness; she traveled overland on horseback through the rugged Allegheny Mountains, then in a wooden boat down the Monongahela, and arrived in Pittsburgh in December 1796. She then traveled by boat down the Ohio and after a brief stay in Marietta arrived in Cincinnati in February 1797. Later that year, the couple moved into a new home in the new town of Ludlow Station, five miles north of Cincinnati. The Ludlow Mansion provided an outpost of civilization on the edge of the frontier.[11]

Charlotte constantly worried about her husband when he was on one of his long survey trips. Ludlow tried to comfort her with descriptions of the lands he saw along the Mad and Great Miami Rivers. In a letter to her father, she related how her husband had told her about these lands with "the beautiful extended plains covered with the most luxuriant vines and strawberries; interspersed with clumps of trees; bounded by lofty forests; diversified by swelling hills; through which flowed the clearest streams. Frequently to this picturesque display, he added flocks of deer, feeding at their ease undisturbed by the presence of man." Ludlow wanted Charlotte to see the wild country and get a taste of "the life of a woodsman," so he made arrangements for them both, accompanied by their two children, two nephews, six men, and a female servant to explore along the Miami and Mad Rivers. Ludlow made sure there were plenty of blankets, provisions, and utensils for cooking. After the trip, Charlotte described the experience in a letter to her father.

> The Mad-river country has the reputation of being the garden-spot of Ohio. The river is neither broad nor deep, but flows with a rapid uniform current over a regular bed of white pebbles, and seldom exceeds its banks. It empties into the Great Miami at the town of Dayton, which Mr. Ludlow has lately laid out, and where he has mills, and other improvements. The Miami also, is a beautiful river. It is not so broad as the Susquehanna, but measured by the scale of utility, it is a finer stream. Mr. Ludlow has land on it also, and has laid out the town of Hamilton near the fort. The river traverses a level, fertile country, and empties into the Ohio, twenty-one miles below Cincinnati.[12]

By the end of 1803, Ludlow and his team had surveyed a large portion of the land between the Miami Rivers, thereby preparing it for settlement. In November 1803 Ludlow resurveyed Township 2, Range 8, which included the west half of Huffman Prairie. Soon afterward he returned home, ill. He attempted to compile his survey notes from that year, but his fever became progressively worse. He wrote an update to Surveyor General Rufus Putnam on January 15, 1804.

> Doubtless you have expected the returns of the surveys committed to myself before this. The surveys are made but I have not quite completed the copying of the field notes and maps; I will have them prepared sometime in the Month if my health and life is spared; I think I can be at Marietta about the last of the month. Should not have detained them this long but have been indisposed with a fever several weeks which

prevented my application to the surveys. Believe me with much respect and esteem, your obedient humble servant, Israel Ludlow.[13]

Israel Ludlow died six days after writing this letter, on January 21, 1804. He was thirty-nine years old. Charlotte was heartbroken and expressed her feelings to her mother:

TO MRS. CHAMBERS.
Ludlow Station, Feb. 3, 1804.
My dear Mother:—
How shall I begin my mournful communication? Your heart will sympathize but too tenderly and deeply in my afflictions, deprived as I am of the most amiable, affectionate, and indulgent of husbands. I am left alone and stricken to the earth! My children are too young to know their loss, and therefore excite the greater pity. My situation demands the exercise of all my reason and religion. . . . On Tuesday morning, Mr. Ludlow arose in his usual health, and on Saturday he left me for eternity. Oh, he is dead, my mother! He is gone from me forever! Language is inadequate to express the agony of such a moment! . . .
     Write to me, dear mother, words of consolation and advice. May the Lord be with me and my children!
Your afflicted daughter,
C.L.[14]

Israel Ludlow held not only the love of Charlotte but the deep respect of his friends and peers, including many prominent individuals of the period. The subsequent influx of settlers, growth of towns and cities, and conversion of natural habitats to agriculture changed the land. The natural resources fed a growing nation, but at the cost of an ancient and complex mosaic of natural plant and animal habitats that was mostly destroyed by the incoming human population before it understood or learned to appreciate it. Fortunately for later historians and naturalists, the field notes, plat maps, and lists of bearing trees recorded by Ludlow and other surveyors created a valuable snapshot of the presettlement forests and prairies of southwest Ohio.

CHAPTER TWO

Ice, Water, and Fire

The big prairie that Israel Ludlow encountered along the Mad River in 1802 was a product of the region's geology, climate, and ecology. He and his team were standing above an ancient river valley that an extinct river had cut from the limestone bedrock millions of years before and more recently had been filled with the residue of melting continental glaciers.[1]

Below their feet were seven feet of black peat, and below that were more than 150 feet of layers of water-saturated sand and gravel interspersed with thinner layers of clay.[2] The bedrock beneath this buried river valley is sedimentary rock, alternating layers of soft shale and hard limestone, of Ordovician age, laid down about 450 million years ago.[3] These layers were formed when what is now southwest Ohio was oriented near the equator and was covered by a tropical sea full of marine life. Large hurricanes formed in this sea and swept across the region; the waves of these storms eroded the bottom sediments and suspended fine-grained materials. In each storm, the coarser material, including shells of mollusks and pieces of coral, was deposited in a layer along the bottom. As the storm abated, the finer grained materials covered the shell layer, and a layer of mud covered this. Over time, these layers became limestone and shale, sedimentary rocks.[4]

In the latter part of the Ordovician period, colliding continents buckled the land and uplifted what is now southwest Ohio, causing the seas to retreat, and rainfall gave rise to a new system of rivers and streams.[5] Before there was an Ohio River, a river of similar size flowed from what is now West Virginia northwest through Ohio and into Indiana. This extinct river, which geologists now call the Teays, cut large,

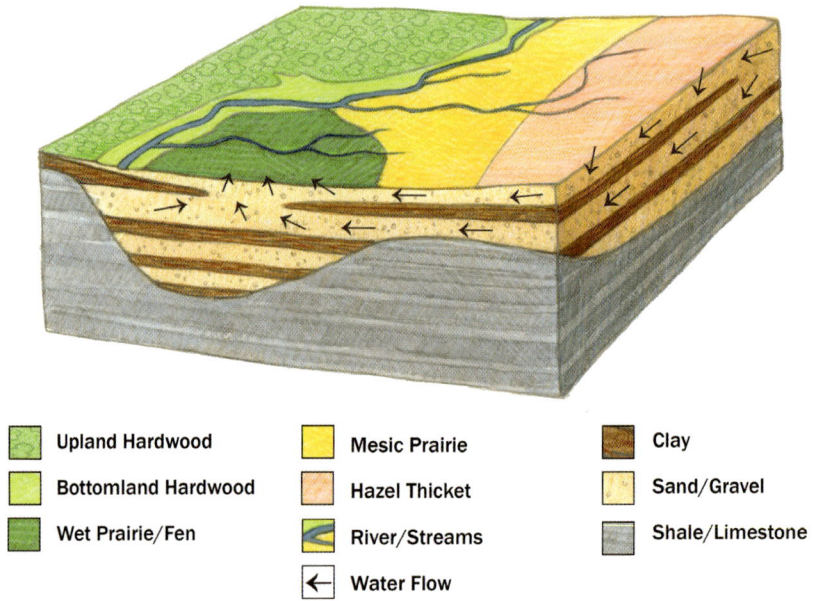

Cutaway illustration of the buried river valley below the presettlement Huffman Prairie. Original artwork by Ann Geise.

🟩	Upland Hardwood	🟨	Mesic Prairie	🟫	Clay
🟩	Bottomland Hardwood	🟧	Hazel Thicket	⬜	Sand/Gravel
🟩	Wet Prairie/Fen	↙	River/Streams	⬜	Shale/Limestone
		←	Water Flow		

deep valleys into the bedrock.[6] The Hamilton River, a large tributary of the Teays, also cut a deep valley below what is now Dayton and Wright-Patterson Air Force Base.[7] About 2 million years ago, an early continental glacier moved south and blocked the flow of the Teays system.[8] The ice wall of the oncoming glacier became a huge dam, backing up rivers and creating large lakes, The current system of rivers became established after the last glacier retreated.

Continental glaciers have descended from the north and covered what is now southwestern Ohio at least four times.[9] Massive amounts of snowfall to the north fed the glaciers.[10] Geologists know the most about the most recent glacier, the Wisconsinan, which buried the work of its predecessors. The Wisconsinan was around 3,000 feet high over what is now Dayton, and moved along at between 55 and 390 feet per year.[11] Like a huge bulldozer, it pulverized and crushed everything above ground level in front of it. This material was then carried along with the ice. As the Wisconsinan moved south, it encountered the Bellefontaine Outlier, a small, hilly area near present-day Bellefontaine that was surrounded by flat land. Like water going around a boulder in a river, the ice sheet broke into two lobes on either side of it. As they moved south, they slowly spread back together again on both sides of the old Hamilton River Valley.[12]

When the climate warmed for a time, the glacier melted as quickly as it advanced. Like a conveyor belt, it deposited the sand, gravel, and

debris it carried into large ridges called moraines. It left other deposits behind when it retreated. Kames were mounds of debris that had gathered in holes in the ice and were deposited when the ice melted. Another type of glacial deposit was composed of gravel that had been deposited along streams within the glacier. This sinuous deposit left behind when glaciers melt is called an esker. A warming climate caused the Wisconsinan glacier to melt away from the Dayton area about sixteen thousand years ago, leaving behind a complex network of moraines, kames, and eskers. These hills are composed of pulverized limestone in the form of sand and gravel and covered in a layer of finer material called glacial till.[13] As the continental glaciers melted north of what is now Dayton, they disgorged a thick stream of rubble and silt called the valley train. This material completely filled the old Hamilton River Valley with layers of gravel, sand, and clay up to 260 feet deep.[14]

The conditions that existed along the front of the glacier and on the barren landscape the glacier left behind when it retreated were conducive to the development of fens, wetlands developed and sustained by the constant flow of cold, limey water flowing from deposits of gravel and sand. These conditions can occur on hillsides; in flat, buried river valleys; or at the edges of natural lakes. Fens do not experience long-term flooding from surface water, they rely on the steady flow of groundwater that saturates the root zone for most of the year.[15] This flow starts with rain falling on the gravel deposits. This water slowly percolates through the gravel and moves downward until it hits something it cannot pass

Eqi Sermia Glacier, Greenland, a scene similar to western Ohio during the Wisconsinan glaciation. Photo by Loraine Tai.

Glacial geology
of southwestern
Ohio. Image
courtesy of Ohio
Geological Survey.

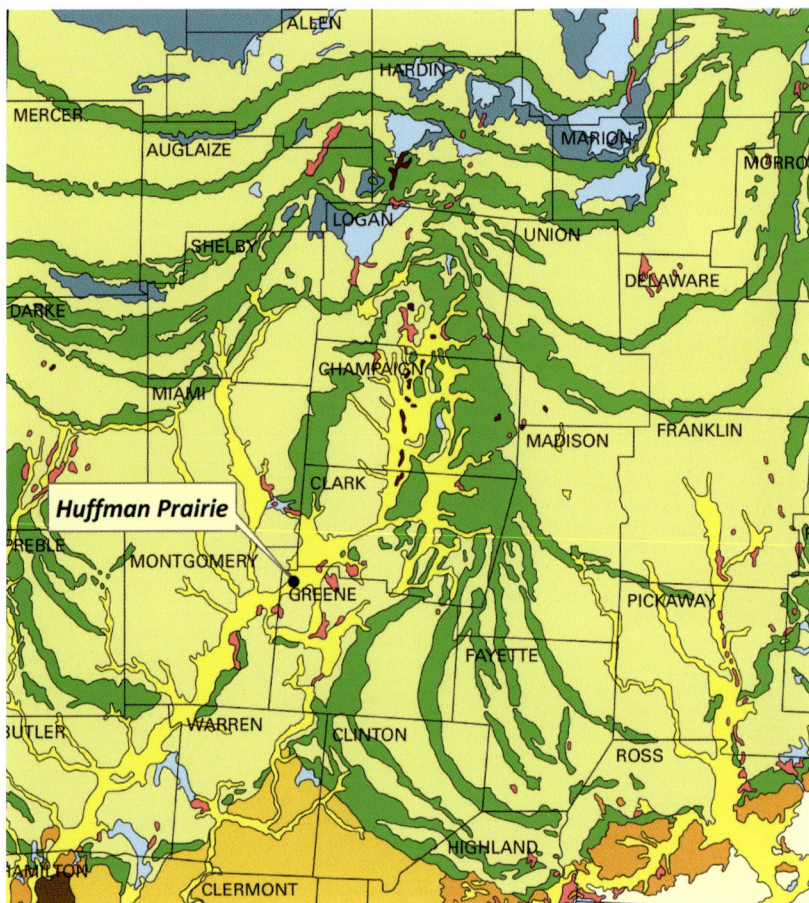

Map courtesy of Ohio Geological Survey, 2005,
Glacial map of Ohio: Ohio Department of Natural Resources,
Division of Geological Survey,
Page-size map with text, 2 p.,
scale 1:2,000,000.

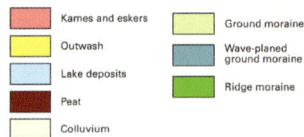

Kames and eskers	Ground moraine
Outwash	Wave-planed ground moraine
Lake deposits	Ridge moraine
Peat	
Colluvium	

through, such as a layer of clay or bedrock. It picks up dissolved calcium carbonate from the limestone gravel as it slowly moves along. Finally, when it flows onto the surface of the ground where the impermeable layer meets the open air, the calcium carbonate dissolved in the water precipitates and forms a light gray, grainy mud called "marl." A patch of exposed marl with a thin layer of groundwater flowing over it is called a marl flat.[16] This is a difficult environment for most plants. Only vegetation adapted to growing where the root zone is constantly saturated with cold, alkaline water can colonize and persist on a marl flat. One of the most successful groups of plants to do so is sedges, grasslike plants with triangular stems, of which there are many species. Some grasses and flowering plants can also tolerate marl flat conditions. When this coloniz-

Marl flat, Heider Fen, Bath Township, Greene County Ohio. Photo by Robert Jurick.

Sedge meadow at Leadingham Prairie Preserve, Medway, Clark County, Ohio.

ing vegetation dies it decomposes very slowly, because of the lack of oxygen in the groundwater and the alkalinity of the marl. Over time, the partially decomposed material builds up and forms the black peat that is characteristic of fens.

Once peat has accumulated, the second zone of a fen, the sedge meadow, takes shape. This distinctive plant community harbors a rich

Above: Queen-of-the-prairie (*Filipendula rubra*) in bloom, Leadingham Prairie Preserve, Medway, Clark County, Ohio.

Above right: Meandering fen stream and shrub-meadow zone, Leadingham Prairie Preserve, Medway, Clark County, Ohio.

Right: Low-gradient cold-water streams were filled with aquatic life like this grass pickerel (*Esox americana*).

diversity of native plant species, such as the beautiful queen-of-the-prairie, and of course, sedges. Fens typically have a third zone, the shrub-meadow zone, dominated by tussocks of waist-high grasses and sedges, thickets of wetland shrubs, and a few trees.[17] Springs that flowed from the marl meadows gathered into increasingly larger channels of cold, clear water that meandered through the wetland.

Fens were likely much more widely distributed in the postglacial environment, becoming scarcer as the climate warmed and the land was colonized by coniferous forests of spruce, pine, and hemlock. Fen plant communities persisted where cold, alkaline water continued to flow from glacial deposits. As the climate continued to warm and the glaciers retreated farther north, deciduous forests of oak, hickory, beech, and other hardwoods replaced the coniferous forests.[18] Even in this new temperate climate, the fens and their postglacial relict plant communities persisted where the necessary flows of cold, alkaline water continued.[19]

From about eight thousand years ago to three thousand years ago, the climate of the Midwest became much hotter and drier. In this period, the Xerothermic or Hypsithermal Interval, prairie grasslands moved eastward and replaced the deciduous forests of western Ohio. North American prairies are chiefly composed of clump-forming grasses and an abundance of flowering plants that reach their peak period of growth in late summer. These prairies came in variations depending on moisture. Wet prairies had their own mix of grasses and flowering plants that thrives in environments where the soil is saturated with water in the winter and early spring but is much drier in the summer. Mesic prairies varied seasonally from moist to dry conditions, and dry, or xeric prairies, became established where soils were dry for most of the year.[20]

The prairies that developed in southwestern Ohio had a unique composition. While many species invaded from the west during the Hypsi-

Restored mesic prairie at Huffman Prairie State Natural Landmark, Greene County, Ohio.

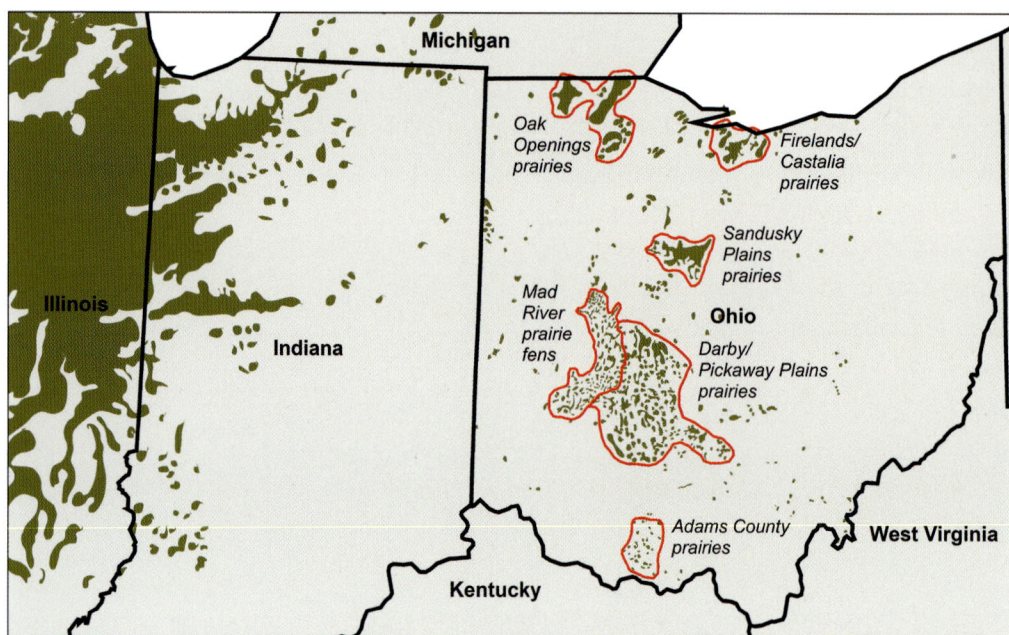

Major prairie regions of Ohio.

thermal Interval, southeastern species invaded as well. For instance, western prairies, such as those in Illinois and Wisconsin, often contain prairie blazing star (*Liatris pycnostachya*) and rosinweed (*Silphium integrifolium*). Both are showy forbs, or flowering plants, that bloom in the summer. These species are not found in southwestern Ohio; they are replaced by the similar spiked blazing star (*Liatris spicata*) and whorled rosinweed (*Silphium trifoliatum*), both southeastern species.

During the Hypsithermal Interval, the fens, or at least some of them, remained where there was a continuous flow of cold groundwater. The diverse fen plant communities mixed with the colonizing prairie species creating a new, even more diverse plant community. The modified fens of southwestern Ohio and the upper Midwest are often called prairie fens.[21] Ohio's prairie fens can contain over five hundred species of plants.[22] They were often part of a mosaic of plant communities that varied with the amount of moisture present: fens transitioned to wet prairies, which graded from mesic to dry prairies.

Three thousand years ago, the climate of southwestern Ohio began changing again, becoming cooler and wetter. Hardwood trees invaded the prairies, and the grasslands shrank over time. By the time the land was settled by Europeans, the prairies had shrunk to scattered islands

surrounded by forests. The larg-
est patches of remaining prairies
were located in the oak openings
of the Toledo area, the Sandusky
Plains near Upper Sandusky, the
Darby and Pickaway plains west
of Columbus, and the Mad River
prairie fens in the valley of that
river. The valley of the Mad River,
also known as the Mad River
Interlobate Ecoregion, was rich
in prairie fens due to the abundance of glacial deposits and the
deeply buried river valley there.[23]

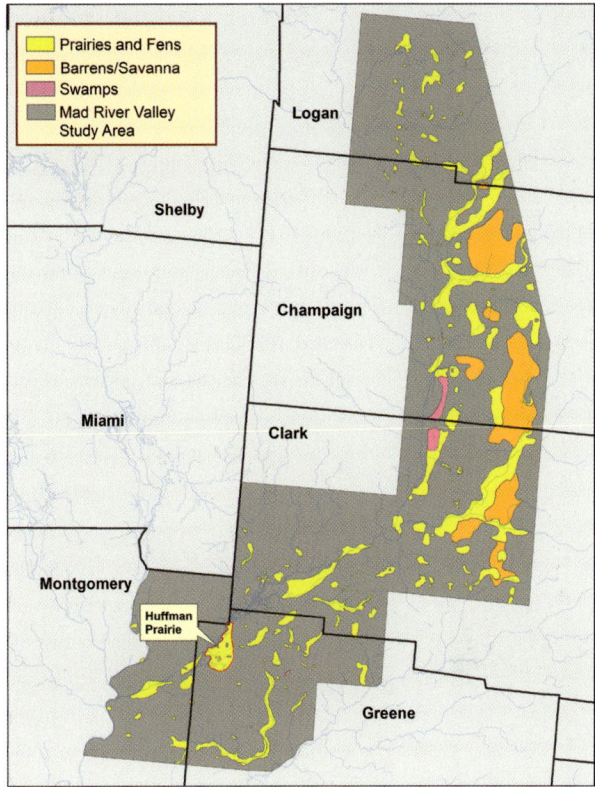

Prairies, fens, and
barrens of the
Mad River Valley
circa 1802.

A study of surveyor records
from the Mad River Valley shows
the scattered distribution of prairie and fen plant communities.[24]
These islands of remaining prairie
likely retained qualities that dis-
couraged trees and favored non-
woody plants: soils that were wet in spring and dry in summer, cold alkaline fens, thin soil over bedrock or gravel, and slopes facing south or
southwest. However, a significant body of evidence suggests that many
of these prairies had lived beyond their time due to regular fires Native
Americans intentionally set.

Humans arrived in North America between fifteen thousand and
twenty-five thousand years ago; prior to that, oceans prevented their
arrival. When a continental glacier was at its peak, much of the world's
water was tied up in ice. This caused sea levels to lower, and a land
bridge would form between Alaska and Siberia, which permitted humans and a variety of mammals to enter North America.[25] Human
populations reached southwestern Ohio not long after the Wisconsinan
glacier retreated.

Successive groups of peoples, each with its own cultures and traits,
have lived in the vicinity of Huffman Prairie. Modern archaeologists
have divided the time that these native peoples have lived in North
America into seven periods: Paleoindian, Archaic, Early Woodland,
Middle Woodland, Late Woodland, Late Prehistoric, and Historic.[26]
Within these, distinct cultures have been identified and studied, such

as the Adena of the Early Woodland period, the Hopewell of the Middle Woodland period, and the Fort Ancient of the Late Prehistoric period. All that is known about them has come from studying artifacts they left behind, some of which have been found in modern times on Huffman Prairie. A 1994–95 study by an archaeological firm discovered eight prehistoric archaeological sites on the prairie. Of these, six were of an unknown origin, one was attributed to the Woodland period, and one the Late Woodland period.[27]

The Shawnee, who may have been descendants of the prehistoric Fort Ancient people, were the Native Americans whom the early settlers of Greene County encountered, for the most part. Under pressure from colonizing Europeans, many of these people had abandoned villages on the Scioto River and moved westward, establishing new ones along the Little Miami and Mad Rivers sometime after 1764.[28] In the late 1700s, they apparently had a small village on Huffman Prairie, but they had been driven away before the town of Mercer's Station was established on this village site in 1794.[29]

The widespread accounts of Native Americans setting fires in prairies and forests throughout the continent indicate that this form of land management was a common practice in much of North America when the land was settled and likely long before that.[30] They lit prairie fires to kill small trees and invigorate growth of prairie grasses, creating nutritious plant life sought by large game such as bison, elk, and white-tailed deer.[31] Native Americans would light prairie fires to drive game to specific locations, where waiting hunters ambushed the animals. Also, a brush-free forest made travel simpler and prey easier to approach. Adriaen van der Donck wrote about Native American burning in New York in 1656:

> The Indians have a yearly custom (which some of our Christians have also adopted) of burning the woods, plains and meadows in the fall of the year, when the leaves have fallen, and when the grass and vegetable substances are dry. Those places which are then passed over are fired in the spring in April. This practice is named by us and the Indians, "bush burning," which is done for several reasons; first, to render hunting easier as the bush and vegetable growth renders the walking difficult for the hunter, and the crackling of the dry substances betrays him and frightens away the game. Secondly, to thin out and clear the woods of all dead substances and grass, which grow better the ensuing spring. Thirdly, to circumscribe and enclose the game within the lines

of the fire, when it is more easily taken, and also, because the game is more easily tracked over the burned parts of the woods.[32]

Another account of intentional burning was made in 1693 by a French missionary and explorer, Father Louis Hennepin, near what is now the Michigan–Indiana border:

Having past through great marshes, we found a vast Plain, on which nothing grows but only some Herbs, which were dry at that time, and burnt, because the bliami's set them on fire every Year, in their hunting wild Bulls (bison), as I shall mention anon. . . . When the Savages discover a great Number of those Beasts together, they likewise assemble their whole Tribe to encompass the Bulls, and then set on fire the dry Herbs about them, except in some places, which they leave free; and therein lay themselves in Ambuscade. The Bulls seeing the Flame round about them, run away through those passages where they see no fire; and there fall into the Hands of the Savages, who by these Means will kill sometimes above six-score in a day.[33]

Colonel James Smith was captured by Delaware Indians in 1755 and adopted by the Mohawk tribe. He wrote a detailed account of his experiences living with the Indians, describing, for example, a ring hunt in the Sandusky Plains of what is now Marion and Crawford Counties, Ohio:

We came to the great meadows or prairies that lie between Sandusky and Sciota. When we came to this place we met with some Ottawa hunters, and agreed with them to take, what they call ring hunt, in partnership. We waited until the expected rain was near falling to extinguish the fire, and then we kindled a large circle in the prairie. At this time, or before the bucks began to run great number of deer lay concealed in the grass, in the day, and moved about in the night; but as the fire burned in towards the centre of the circle, the deer fled before the fire: The Indians were scattered also at some distance before the fire, and shot them down every opportunity, which was very frequent, especially as the circle became small. When we came to divide the deer, there were above ten to each hunter, which were all killed in few hours. The rain did not come on that night to put out the out-side circle of the fire, and as the wind arose, it extended thro the whole prairie, which was about fifty miles in length, and in some places near twenty in breadth.[34]

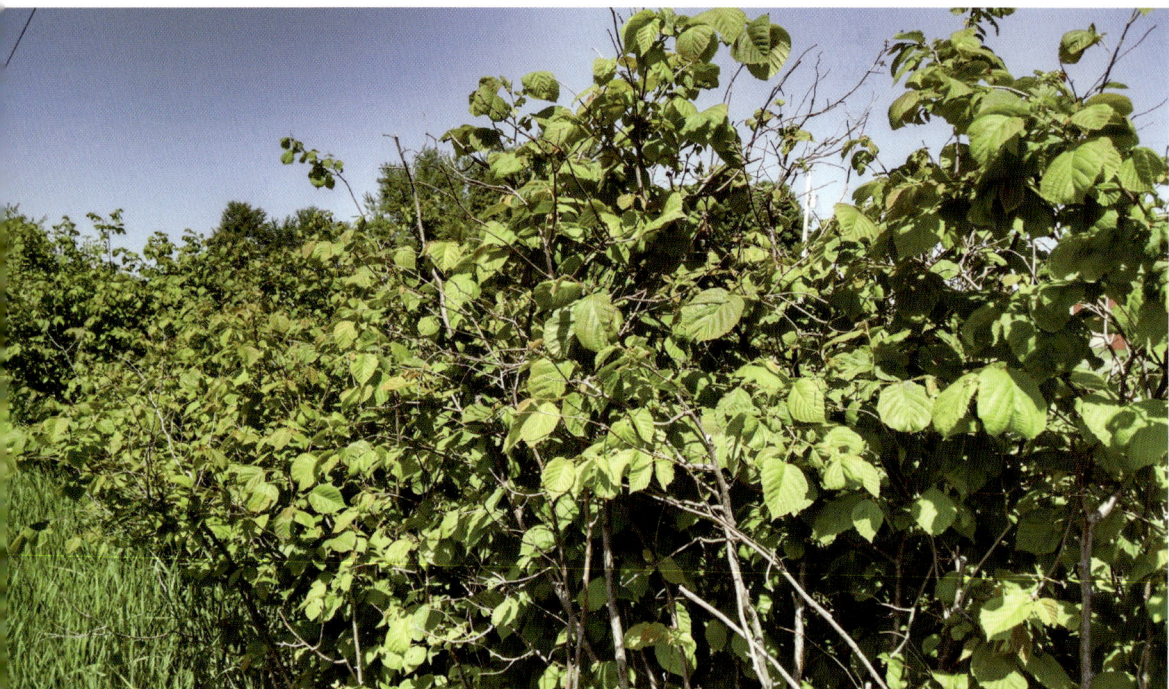

Above: Thicket of American hazelnut (*Corylus americana*), Prairie Grass Multiuse Trail, Clark County, Ohio. Field notes of early surveyors indicate that in 1802–3 extensive thickets of American hazelnut, wild plum, and young oaks bordered Huffman Prairie on the east side.

Right: Presettlement vegetation and streams of western Bath Township, Greene County Ohio.

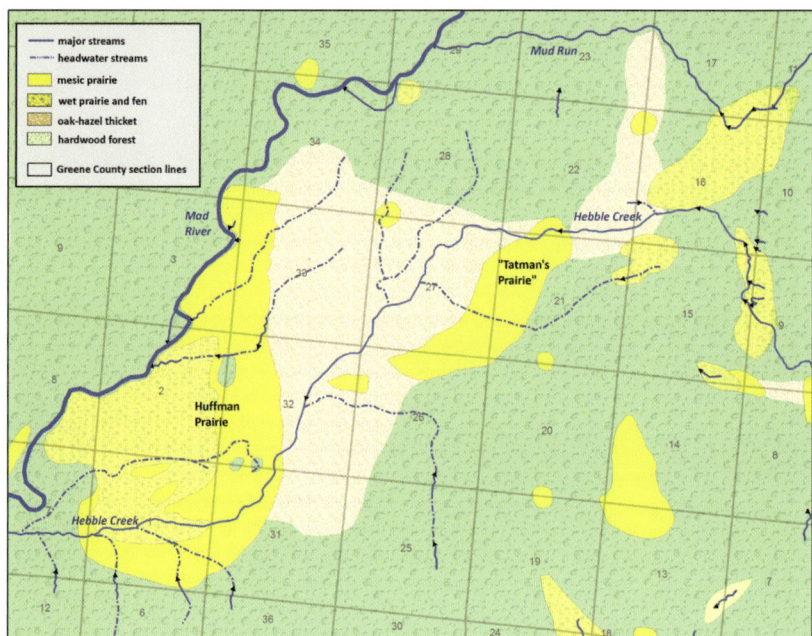

These and many other similar accounts indicate that the native peoples who lived in North America, including southwestern Ohio, were not merely accepting the land as they found it, they were its active managers, primarily by their use of fire. This land management practice was responsible for a significant portion of the biodiversity and natural beauty that early settlers found in Ohio's prairie regions. Ohio's prairies were formed and maintained initially by the advent of a favorable climate, but burning added another dimension of complexity to the landscape. Frequent, large-scale prairie fires set by Native Americans also burned into surrounding forests, killing trees to varying degrees. This process created new plant communities somewhere between prairie and forest, which were documented by early surveyors, who called them barrens and oak openings.

Indian fires had evidently decreased or ceased in the Huffman Prairie region in the decades prior to the first land surveys. When Ludlow surveyed the Huffman Prairie region in 1802 and 1803, another large prairie, later known as Tatman's Prairie, was one mile east.[35] The land between these two prairies was covered by poorly timbered land, dominated by American hazelnut, wild plum, and young oaks. It seems plausible that these extensive oak-hazel thickets had recently been prairie but had become overgrown with these woody species due to the decrease or cessation of fires. If so, then Huffman Prairie had recently been much larger, up to six thousand acres.

CHAPTER THREE

Early Exploration and Settlement

Frontiersman Christopher Gist is the first person to give a written description of the prairies of southwestern Ohio. In September 1750, the governor of Virginia engaged him to "search out and discover the Lands upon the river Ohio, & other adjoining branches of the Mississippi down as low as the great falls thereof." In February 1751, as part of this expedition, Gist traveled from the Shawnee town called "Shannoah" near what is now Portsmouth, Ohio to the "Twigtwee Town," near what is now Piqua, on the Great Miami River. On this journey, Gist made a detailed description of what he observed, including the prairies in what are now Greene, Clark, and Champaign Counties:

Sunday February 17.—Crossed the little Miamee River, and altering our Course. We went S W 25 M to the Big Miamee River, opposite the Twig-twee Town. All the way from the Shannoah Town to this Place (except the first 20 M which is broken) is rich fine and Level Land, well Timbered with large Walnut, Ash, Sugar Trees, Cherry Trees &c, it is well watered with a great Number of little Streams or Rivulets, and full of beautiful natural Meadows, covered with wild Rye, Blue Grass and clover, and abounds with Turkeys Deer, and Elks and most sorts of Game particularly Buffaloes, thirty or forty of which are frequently seen feeding in one meadow: In short nothing but Cultivation to make it a most delightful Country.

   Sunday March 3.—. . . . , I left the Path and went to the South West-ward down the little Miamee River or Creek, where I had fine travelling through rich Land and beautiful Meadows, in which I could sometimes see forty or fifty Buffaloes feeding at once—The Little Miamee River or

Above: A scene similar to the one Christopher Gist saw in southwest Ohio in 1751. Photo by Artush/ Shutterstock.

Right: Benjamin Van Cleve, image from Augustus Waldo Drury, *History of the City of Dayton and Montgomery County, Ohio,* vol. 1 (Dayton, Ohio: S. J. Clarke, 1909), 63

Creek continued to run the Middle of a fine Meadow, about a mile wide clear like an Old Field and not a Bush in it, I could see the Buffaloes in it above two miles off.[1]

The first documented reference to what came to be called Huffman Prairie was made by a young pioneer named Benjamin Van Cleve in 1795. Van Cleve was sixteen when he arrived in Cincinnati in 1790 with his parents and five siblings. The next year, Native Americans killed his father, John, at the family home in Cincinnati. Thereafter, Benjamin assumed responsibility for the family and engaged in numerous activities to support them.[2]

In September 1795, Benjamin joined a surveying expedition to what is now Montgomery and Greene Counties. A few weeks before, four investors—General Arthur St. Clair, governor of the Northwest Territory; General Jonathan Dayton; General James Wilkinson; and Israel Ludlow—had purchased from John Cleves Symmes a large tract of wilderness containing the seventh and eighth ranges between the Great and Little Miami Rivers, including the big prairie along the Mad River. Two parties left Cincinnati to survey the land. One team was to mark a new road to a proposed town site where the Mad River met the Great Miami, later called the Mad River Road.[3] The second team, led by Captain John Dunlap, was to survey the tract's boundary. Benjamin kept a detailed journal of his adventure:

I never having seen this part of the country, my object was to see as much of it as I could, and, knowing Captain Dunlap's party would have the best opportunity, I went with him . . . 26th. This morning our horse was gone and probably stolen by some Indians, as he had been well secured. This day was very rainy, and we did nothing except hunt our horse to no purpose.

27th. We carried our baggage up to the mouth of Mad river and soon after Mr. Cooper and his party arrived. We found six Wyandot Indians here, who encamped about thirty perches above us on the bank of Mad River, which they called Chillicothe River [now Deed's Point MetroPark]. They were very friendly. They gave us two pieces of venison jerk and we, being scarce of provisions as well as themselves, would not give them much. However, we gave them some flour and salt and a little tobacco. They wanted almost everything we had and more. One of them fancied my knife and gave me his knife and belt and a deer skin for mine.

28th. Some Kentucky landjobbers that came with Cooper made a small tour of about two miles above the mouth (of Mad river) through the overgrown and prairie land, and finding it not according to their expectations, returned for home. Mr. Cooper not having finished the road to his mind concluded to return and finish it and leave us to perform the business. Meandered a small distance down the Miami. [This means the party followed the river bank downstream on foot.]

29th. Came to our third mile stake on our line to the Little Miami.

30th. We came to a large creek afterward called Beaver creek, which we mistook for the Little Miami, and found the distance to be nine miles and ten chains east from our north meridian line [near current Alpha, Ohio].

October 1st. Ran from our last stake north nine miles and a half through some very fine prairie and good wood land. Encamped on a very pretty creek [now Mud Run].

2d. Struck Mad river, running nearly west, at ten miles and seventy chains. We had to offset to the east two miles and a half to get our distance—twelve miles north. Then meandered down the river. We sent our hunter (Wm. Gahagan) and pack-horse man (Jonathan Mercer) down below us to cook against we came, but, unluckily, they fell in with some Indians, who robbed them of nearly all our flour.

3d. We continued meandering nearly all this day, a prairie to our left [Huffman Prairie]. 4th. Came to the mouth [now Deeds Point] and finished meandering the river. Came through prairie all this day. Rained very hard. We had to secure our field notes and I cut the bearings and distances on a large chip with my knife, not being able to keep paper dry about us.

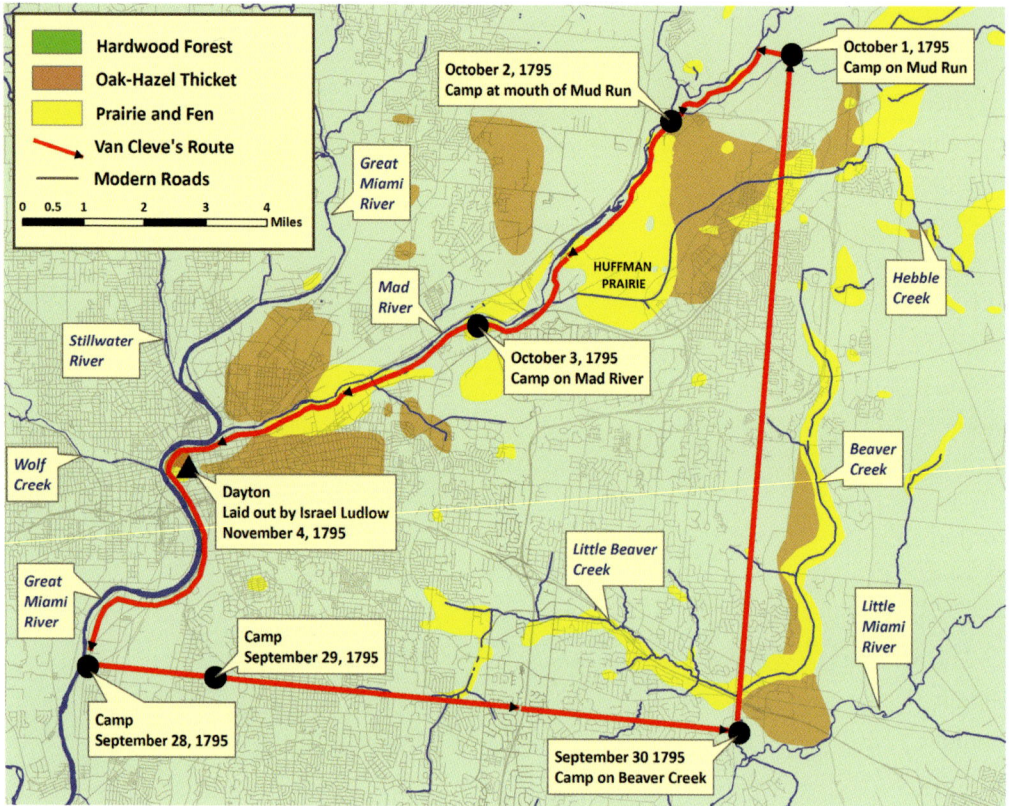

The route of Benjamin Van Cleve's adventure through the prairies of northwest Greene County in 1795.

On November 1, the surveyors returned to the mouth of the Mad River. Here Israel Ludlow led a survey for the plat for the new town, naming it Dayton after fellow investor Jonathan Dayton.[4]

In the spring of 1796 three groups left Cincinnati to settle the uninhabited town site. The first included Van Cleve's surveying companion Jonathan Mercer and his brother Edward Mercer, both from Virginia. They took a circuitous overland route and were the last to arrive. A second group, of nineteen people, set out in a long, narrow wooden boat called a pirogue, up the Great Miami River. Benjamin Van Cleve and William Gahagan, who were each provided a pole with a heavy socket and placed on either side of the boat, powered and steered it. They "set their poles near the head of the boat and bringing the end of the pole to their shoulders, with their bodies bent, walked slowly down the running board to the stern, returning at a quick pace to the bow for the new set."[5] This party was the first to arrive at what would become Dayton, on April 1. The third group, including Benjamin's brother William Van Cleve, went overland, making a difficult journey by wagon down the partially blazed road cut the year before.[6]

Benjamin became a prominent citizen of the new town. He was the first schoolteacher, clerk of the court, librarian, and postmaster before he died in 1821 at the age of forty-eight.[7] Benjamin's sister Margaret remained in Cincinnati. Her daughter Catharine married Daniel Wright, and their son Milton was the father of Orville and Wilbur Wright.[8]

Soon after arriving in Dayton, Jonathan and Edward Mercer "with all their worldly possessions in the panniers of one horse, went on up Mad River several miles, and located on prairie land that is now in Bath Township, Greene County."[9] Here they established a settlement on the north end of Huffman Prairie, calling it Mercer's Station. One account placed the town "one and one-half miles south of the present village of Osborn, on a parcel owned and occupied by James Williamson."[10] If accurate, this would place Mercer's Station in the northwest quarter of Section 33, in the vicinity of what is now Bass Lake on Wright-Patterson Air Force Base. Mercer's Station was threatened by Indians several times, and on one occasion the residents fled back to Dayton for safety.[11]

The Mercers, like the original settlers of Dayton, had purchased their land from Arthur St. Clair, Jonathan Dayton, James Wilkinson, and Israel Ludlow, who had together purchased the tract from John Cleves Symmes. Unfortunately for the settlers of Dayton and Mercer's Station, the United States discovered that Symmes had been selling more land than he had actually paid for, and these pioneers had become squatters on land they did not actually own. Hoping to solve the problem, Benjamin Van Cleve and Daniel Cooper wrote a testimonial to the U.S. Congress, signed by the settlers who had invested so much of their time and resources:

To the Honorable Senate and House of Representatives of the United States in Congress Assembled:

. . ."On the 5th of November, 1795, forty-six persons engaged to become settlers at Dayton, but from the many difficulties in forming a new settlement so far in a wilderness country, only fifteen of those came forward, with four others, making nineteen in all. From the threats and ill-treatment of the savages to the people of Mercer's Station it was once evacuated, and at several times Mr. Mercer with two brothers maintained the station at the risk of their lives. These settlements were formed by your petitioners a few months after the treaty of Greenville, when we had not faith in the friendship of the savages. Our settlement was immediately on their hunting grounds. We were not able to keep a horse amongst us during the first season, by reason of their stealing. The scarcity of provisions had raised flour to nine dollars a barrel, and

TRACT	PATENT DATE	BUYER(S)	ACRES
1	7-2-1827	James Williamson, assignee of John Brake	150
2	6-30-1812	James and William Williamson, assignees of Jesse Rush	160
3	2-7-1817	William Short, assignee of William Barr and George Torrence	166
4	12-6-1821	William Williamson	160
5	10-10-1827	A. Irwin and L. Whiteman	65
6	10-10-1827	Robert E. Stephen	80
8	6-6-1809	James McCormick	94
9	11-1-1830	Elnathan Cory	179
10	11-1-1830	Elnathan Cory	80
11	11-1-1830	Benjamin Stiles	80
12	6-27-1817	Jesse Hunt	160
13	5-6-1819	William Huffman, assignee of Jonathan Clayton	166
14	4-12-1821	William Huffman of Dayton	320
15	8-29-1812	Samuel Stiles	243
16	6-10-1813	Jacob Cutler, Assignee of Benjamin Chambers	160
17	6-16-1817	Heirs of Jonathan Mercer, late of Hamilton County	320
18	10-10-1816	Anthony M. Cozard, John Cozard, Assignes of Thomas Newport	160

Original land
patents on
Huffman Prairie,
1809–30.

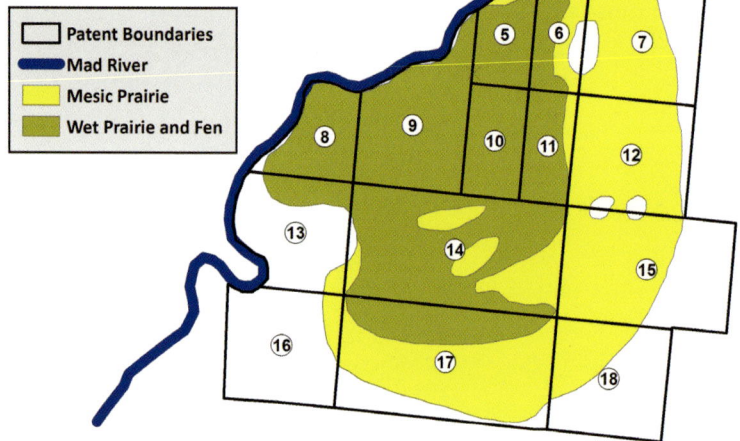

Patent Boundaries
Mad River
Mesic Prairie
Wet Prairie and Fen

other articles in proportion, which we had to purchase and transport fifty miles through a wilderness, clearing roads, etc.; under all these and many more difficulties we labored in hopes of obtaining our lands at a low rate and the small gratuity offered . . . we pray that congress will make to us such gratuity in lands, or deduction from payments of land, or grant such other relief as our case merits."[12]

Congress's solution to this problem was to pass relief acts that gave these original settlers preemption rights that gave them the ability to repurchase the land they now occupied. These preemption lands had to be identified, and the task fell to Israel Ludlow to survey them, which he did in 1803. Citizens with preemption rights in this area had the first right to buy their land from the federal government, for $2 per acre.[13] However, most of the Dayton and Mercer's Station settlers did not have the necessary funds or feel inclined to purchase their land a second time. Nearly all of them gave up and left, and the new settlements were in danger of disappearing altogether. In Dayton, Daniel C. Cooper solved the problem by purchasing the preemption rights from the few remaining original settlers, as well as the rest of the lots in the town. When Cooper subsequently sold the land, the new owners received clear titles.[14] Mercer's Station had no benefactor and ceased to exist as a town, but new settlers subsequently platted the village of Fairfield, one and a half miles to the east, in 1816.[15]

In 1800, the U.S. Congress passed the Harrison Land Act, which established federal land offices in Steubenville, Chillicothe, and Cincinnati, making it easier to buy newly surveyed lands.[16] After a piece of land was purchased at a land office, the owner was issued a land patent, signed by the president of the United States, that described the property, named the buyer, and confirmed receipt of payment.[17] The big prairie along the Mad River east of Dayton left the public domain through sales of patents between 1809 and 1830 at the Cincinnati Land Office. As a result of these sales, the wilderness prairie that had prospered as a natural landscape for thousands of years was cut into eighteen rectangular pieces, with each owner having a different vision of how to use the land.

In the 1830s there was an emerging interest in documenting the plant life of the United States, particularly the frontier regions such as Ohio, which held previously unrecorded species. Several noted botanists, often physicians, were active in Ohio and detailed its natural plants and communities.[18] John Leonard Riddell visited Huffman Prairie in 1834 and described five species from there in his 1834 publication "A Synopsis of the Flora of the Western States." A herbarium specimen of Riddell's goldenrod (*Solidago riddellii*) collected at Huffman Prairie became one of two accepted as the first documentation of this species. Riddell's notation confirms his collection location as "Hoffman's Prairie, 8 miles E. from Dayton."[19]

Another new Huffman Prairie species Riddell documented was *Amaranthus miamiensis,* now called *Amaranthus tuberculatus,* the tall waterhemp.[20] Riddell found a third new species in Dayton, the Ohio goldenrod (*Oligoneuron ohioensis*), that he documented in Van Cleve's Prairie, Dayton.[21] Prominent Dayton citizen John Whitten Van Cleve owned this prairie fen, part of his forty-four-acre farm in what is now East Dayton.[22]

John W. Van Cleve, Benjamin's son, was born in 1801, Dayton's first male child.[23] Benjamin was determined to

Riddell's goldenrod (*Solidago riddellii*). Photo by Jim McCormac.

Type specimen of Riddell's goldenrod that J. L. Riddell collected at Huffman Prairie in 1834. Image courtesy of Academy of Natural Sciences of Drexel University, used with permission.

provide John a college education and arranged for him to attend Ohio University in Athens in 1817. Benjamin had a close relationship with his son, as evidenced by this portion of a letter he wrote to John in 1818:

> It will always give pleasure to me, to learn of your doing good and improving. Youth looking forward to the ordinary period of human life, too often misspend this time and neglect the golden opportunity of fitting themselves for usefulness and of doing good here. Days, months and years fly swift away, and when the aged look back life is short, it

is like a dream. He who has improved his time has lived to virtue, has laid hold of the anchor of hope in early life, who after doing all the good he can feel his own unworthiness and dependence and relies on the merits of a blessed Saviour for the rest, can enjoy a happiness and tranquility of mind through life, comfort in death, and confidence of a reward beyond the grave. These are not ideas suggested by a mind enfeebled by indisposition, they are the sober dictates of an imagination maturely determined in health. The advice of a father who values your future felicity more than life. I pray you profit by it.[24]

John Van Cleve took his father's advice. After graduation, he returned to Dayton and began a life of public service and scientific study, particularly geology and botany. Van Cleve was a colorful and important figure in Dayton's early development. He served as recorder in 1824 and 1828; mayor in 1830, 1831, and 1832; and city engineer for several terms. He compiled and lithographed a map of the city in 1839.[25] He envisioned and planned the city's beautiful Woodland Cemetery. His friend Robert Steele later described him as "a born scholar, endowed with a vigorous intellect, remarkable memory, and a facility for acquiring knowledge of both mathematics and languages."[26] He recalled, "He was one of those who call every bush my cousin. Original in character, odd in appearance, the jolly band of children who followed his burly figure through many holiday excursions grew wiser, happier, and healthier." John Van Cleve never married. For many years he lived in a rented room in a tavern in Dayton with his pet crow, Billy, and pet raccoon, Toby.[27] A very large man, he enjoyed leading groups of children through the woods and prairies around Dayton and teaching them about the natural world. He undertook expeditions to destinations such as Huffman Prairie and Clifton Gorge using a horse-drawn bus, or omnibus. This early form of public transportation together with new roads and turnpikes made such adventures possible.

One of the children with whom Van Cleve shared the wilds of Dayton was Lucyanna Greene. Her granddaughter Agnes Anderson Hall compiled a biography of John Van Cleve chiefly from stories her mother and grandmother told her and actual letters Van Cleve had written. One story Lucyanna told her granddaughter was of a trip to Huffman Prairie, where fringed gentians, a beautiful fall flower in prairie fens, were especially common:

When we read about fringed gentians—almost a lost flower in our woods—she would tell us, "John knew a place out on the prairie where

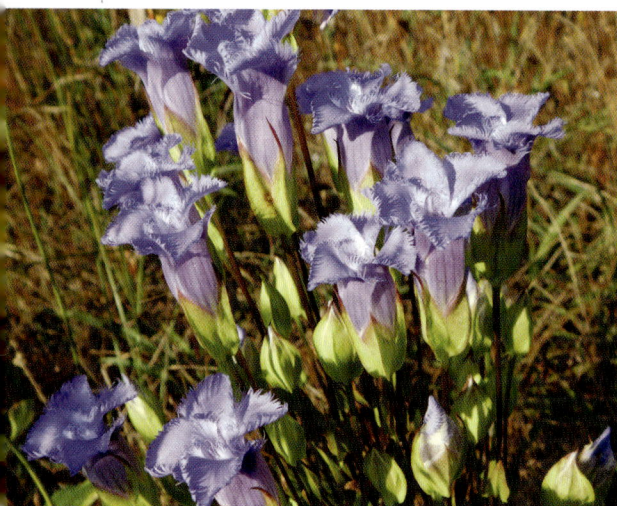

Above: Lesser fringed gentian (*Gentianopsis virgata*).

Right: Herbarium specimen of whorled rosinweed (*Silphium trifoliatum*) collected and mounted by John Van Cleve. Original specimen photographed at Boonshoft Museum of Discovery, Dayton.

they covered the ground with blue when they were in bloom. It was lovely!"

"Did you ever see them growing, yourself?"

"Oh yes, but not very often. John didn't like to take us there because we had to cross a lot of boggy ground where there were rattle-snakes. He thought it was dangerous."

"I thought you said John wasn't afraid of snakes."

"He wasn't. He wasn't afraid of anything for himself, and he always taught us that our common snakes are harmless; but rattle-snakes are different."[28]

In 1832 Van Cleve purchased a copy of botanist John Torrey's book *Compendium of the Flora of Northern and Middle States* for $1.25 and commenced a botanical inventory of the Dayton area.[29] His copy of the compendium is full of his notes in the margins of the book, documenting the species he located.[30] As evidenced by a letter he wrote to John Torrey on August 27, 1838, he took botany very seriously:

Dear Sir,

Your favor of the 4th last has been received, and an opportunity offering,

I send you a few plants, none of them perhaps, but some of them subject to some doubts or uncertainties, on which I should like to have some information. I have numbered the specimens and shall refer to them accordingly in my suggestions or inquiries.

No. 1. Doctor Frank, a German Botanist, who visited this neighborhood called it a Kuhnia, certainly improperly; and other call it Aster Amydalinus, which does not satisfy me. Your edition of 1826 describes that as a foot high and the scales of the calyx lanceolate, obtuse. This plant I have never seen less than three feet high and sometimes it is six. It's only locality here is in wet prairies.

No 2. This beautiful plant I have not been able to determine. It is frequently very branched, 12 to 20 inches high, found in dry prairies.[31]

Van Cleve also made a herbarium of 207 artistically mounted plant specimens, a large portion of them collected in prairies and fens near Dayton, many probably from Huffman Prairie. Upon his death, the herbarium was donated to the Cooper Female Seminary. When the school closed in 1886, Professor William Werthner, a noted teacher and botanist at Dayton's Central High School, acquired the herbarium. Werthner donated it to the Dayton Public Library Museum, which became the Dayton Museum of Natural History. The herbarium was forgotten for many years, until botanist Larry Morse rediscovered it in 1966 while doing an inventory of the museum's botanical collections. After some research, he determined that this herbarium, obviously far older than the other specimens there, was made by Van Cleve. Morse, who later became the chief botanist for The Nature Conservancy, wrote a short article about the herbarium for the museum and gave a presentation on it to the Ohio Academy of Science in 1967.[32] The herbarium remains in this collection, now housed at the Boonshoft Museum of Discovery in Dayton. Van Cleve's book and herbarium document many species that are now rare or no longer found in the Dayton area.

Unfortunately, another of Van Cleve's botanical works was lost, and has not been found: a book of wildflower sketches called "Beauties of Flora." A good description of this lost work was included in Hall's "Letters from John":

It is a beautiful volume, bound in black leather with a border of leaves in gold edging it. We have been told that John bound it himself. The covers are centered by inserts in red, also bordered with gold tracery, the front one bearing the inscription "Beauties of Flora." . . . The whole book

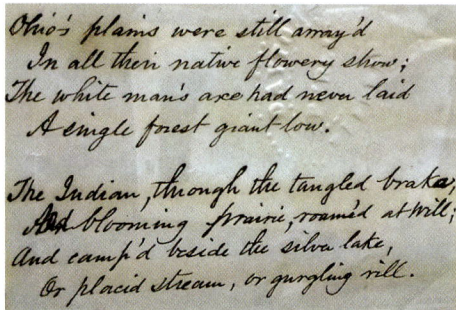

Untitled poem by John Van Cleve. Original in Dayton Metro Library Genealogy Center, Van Cleve–Dover Collection.

is an exquisite piece of work. Done when exactitude in line, color and detail were demanded of an artist, the very veins of the leaves and petals are traced almost as if by Nature's own hand. The petals are delicately shaded and the soft gray shadow back of each spray of flower and leaf gives the impression of life to an almost startling degree. Every flower is marked with its Latin and English names in infinitesimal letters, the Latin names in one kind of script—the English in another, and the skill of John's fingers is demonstrated again in that marking.[33]

Another example of Van Cleve's appreciation for the beauty of the prairies and forests near early Dayton is this untitled poem, written in his distinctive handwriting:

> Ohio's plains were still array'd
>   In all their native flowery show;
> The white man's axe had never laid
>   A single forest giant low.
>
> The Indian, through the tangled brake,
>   And blooming prairie, roamed at will;
> And camp'd beside the silver lake,
>   Or placid stream, or gurgling rill.[34]

In the early 1830s, Dayton and the other towns in the Miami Valley largely remained outposts in the wilderness, mainly because there was no network of good roads to support farming, travel, and open markets. To solve the problem, the State of Ohio granted charters to private turnpike companies. These companies raised the necessary funds by selling stocks. When the turnpike was completed, the companies would charge tolls to cover costs and repay the investors.[35] Local citizens formed the Dayton and Springfield Turnpike Company to connect the two towns, and the road was constructed in 1838. This turnpike, which bisected Huffman Prairie between Dayton and Fairfield, contained bridges, stone culverts, tollgates, milestones, and comfortable brick taverns.[36] The next turnpike to cross Huffman Prairie was the Byron, Yellow Springs and Clifton, which was incorporated in 1845 and was built shortly thereafter.[37] In 1851, the Dayton & Springfield Railway, later known as the Mad River

& Lake Erie Railroad, was built through the prairie.[38] All of these transportation routes made access to the prairie easier and made it possible to begin converting its rich soils to agricultural production.

In 1812, William Hoffman; his wife, Lydia; and their five children set out from Monmouth County, New Jersey, to the young town of Dayton, Ohio, arriving there in May. In Dayton, the spelling of the name was changed to "Huffman."[39] The Huffmans built a stone house, the first one in Dayton, on Jefferson and Third Streets; it served as dwelling and general store. William was a successful merchant and land speculator.[40] One of his real estate projects started with the purchase of a land patent on a 166-acre tract of prairie eight miles east of Dayton on

Early roads, railroads, and ditches on Huffman Prairie. Background map by A. E. Rogerson and E. J. Murphy, from *1855 Atlas Map of Greene County, Ohio* (Philadelphia: Anthony D. Byles, 1855), courtesy of Library of Congress Geography and Map Division.

May 6, 1819. On April 12, 1821, he expanded his prairie holdings with the purchase of an additional 320 acres to the east of the first tract.[41]

William's son, William P., took an active interest in his father's wild prairie land. In 1837, at age twenty-four, he moved to the prairie and built a house there. That fall, he married Anna Tate; they lived on the prairie for ten years and did their best to turn it into a farm. In 1848 William P., Anna, and their five children moved back to Dayton.[42] There, he became active in numerous business and real estate ventures as well as civic projects to help the growing city. He was one of the incorporators of the Second National Bank, in 1863, and its president for many years. He was president of the Third National Bank from its organization up to 1887. He invested much energy in public infrastructure projects, including the Third Street Railway, the Dayton and Springfield Pike, and the Cooper Hydraulic Company. He was also a member of the board of trustees of Denison University and served as president of the Woodland Cemetery Association.[43] After returning to Dayton, he and Anna had five more children. He also purchased tracts on the prairie that came up for sale.

In 1860 the U.S. Census Bureau compiled a tally of the agricultural assets of landowners. This tally, known as an agricultural schedule,

Dayton and Springfield Turnpike near Huffman Prairie in 1918. Image courtesy of the Miami Conservancy District.

65-392
7-18

shows the progress William P. made in converting his section of Huffman Prairie to agricultural use between 1837 and 1860. These records indicate that some three hundred acres of the wild prairie remained on Huffman's farm in 1860, but more than five hundred acres were being cultivated with a mix of crops or used for providing hay or pasture for livestock.[44] When William P. died in 1888, his land holdings passed to his sons Frank, Torrence, George, and William.[45] In 1898, their combined holdings on the prairie totaled 1,223 acres.[46]

The main stream that flowed across Huffman Prairie, Hebble Creek, has its origins in eastern Bath Township, obtaining its flow from several high-volume springs that originate in glacial kames.[47] Prior to the 1950s, this small stream was known as Three Springs Run. Israel Ludlow described it as "beautiful" and in his 1803 field notes wrote how it "affords much water."[48] This stream flowed along the north and west ends of the new town of Fairfield, which was platted in 1816, from where it ran southwest across Huffman Prairie to the Mad River.[49]

In 1815, Jacob Smith, a man with milling experience, started acquiring land and the necessary water rights to establish a water-powered gristmill in Fairfield, about a mile and a half east of Huffman Prairie. Smith, an early Greene County pioneer, was also one of the first Greene County commissioners, and a senator representing Greene County in the state legislature, where he served nine one-year terms.[50] Smith died in 1819, and the mill and water rights passed to his wife and children. The Fairfield Mill was constructed between 1820 and 1831, but it does not seem to have been a big success. The mill does not appear on county tax records

Fairfield Mill, circa 1920. Image courtesy of Ann Armstrong-Ingoldsby.

Eleanor Black standing on the dam of the Fairfield Mill, the millpond behind her, about 1920. Photo by Inez Armstrong, image courtesy of Ann Armstrong-Ingoldsby.

from that time, and Smith's estate included many debts.[51] In 1831, the mill was purchased by a miller from Miami County named Robert C. Crawford, who turned it into a successful business.[52] In 1832, Crawford purchased or built a second gristmill on Hebble Creek two and one-half miles upstream of the Fairfield Mill.[53] He successfully operated both mills until his death in 1842. The Fairfield Mill operated until the mid-1920s.

In the days of Smith and Crawford, much of the land was still a wilderness. Local landowners were anxious to establish a successful gristmill in the community.[54] However, the modified streams and millraces were designed to supply water to the mill, not control flooding. As the land was settled and farms were established, the flooding of land adjacent to millraces became more of an issue. This was the case on Huffman

Prairie, where flooding and poor drainage became a concern for a farmer named Jacob Frick. On December 6, 1864, Frick petitioned the Greene County commissioners to construct a new ditch to drain his farm on Huffman Prairie. Frick and his attorney, A. W. Dewey, blamed the flooding on the Fairfield Mill and the waters of its tailrace:

> To the Honorable Board of County Commissioners within and for the County of Greene in the State of Ohio. The undersigned your petitioner respectfully represents that he is the owner of land situate in the Township of Bath, in said County, that a large proportion of his said lands are overflowed and rendered useless and unavailable for agricultural purpose by the waters of the mill race of the Fairfield Mill in said township and county. . . . The necessity of a ditch or drain through this part of the country is evinced from the fact that all the water used to propel two run of burrs at the Fairfield Mills; and also the drainage between said mills and S. E. Bennett's south line is poured into the low grounds along the line of this ditch or drain, while the trifling ditch already constructed is quite inadequate to carry off so large an amount of water, the natural consequence is that the water in an ordinary wet season rushes down into the low lands in quantities too large for the present ditch and spreads over the low grounds, and remains there until absorbed by the earth, or evaporated by the rays of the sun causing material injury to the health of the inhabitants within its metanous influences and rendering unavailable for agricultural purposes a large amount of excellent land which would be exceedingly valuable were there a ditch of proper dimensions made through these lands.[55]

Frick was probably off base to blame the Fairfield Mill for his flooding problems: the mill did not produce water; it just used it. His concerns about drainage dumping just upstream of his farm, however, were probably justified. The Bath Township trustees had mandated the installation or expansion of several ditches on Hebble Creek. These projects—known as the "Kiefer-Brannum Ditch" (1854), "Cosad Ditch" (1854), and "Herring Ditch" (1859)—collected and drained runoff from these farms, and discharged it upstream of Frick's farm.[56]

However, Frick's petition was successful, and in 1865 the "Frick Ditch" was approved for construction by the Greene County commissioners. The ditch essentially channelized Hebble Creek between the Fairfield Mill tailrace and the Mad River. It crossed the lands of eleven Huffman Prairie landowners, including William P. Huffman; each had to pay the assessment to build the ditch across his land or use his own resources

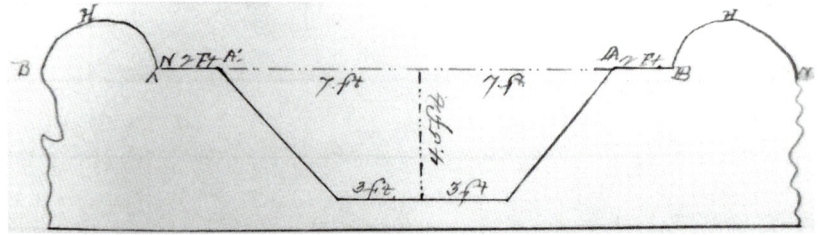

Cross section of Frick Ditch as modified in 1873. Photographed from Greene County Archives, Ditch Records, 2:5.

Existing ditch on Wright-Patterson Air Force Base along Hebble Creek Road. Huffman Prairie State Natural Landmark is in the background. Ditch dimensions and course similar to Frick Ditch, installed in 1865.

to construct the ditch. Huffman elected to dig the ditch across his land with his own resources, and he was supposed to have this accomplished by July 1, 1865. The task was not completed on time, and Huffman received a terse letter from W. L. M. Baker, the Greene County auditor. Baker informed Huffman that his portion of the ditch would be "let at public outcry" in front of the Greene County courthouse to the lowest bidder, at 2 P.M. on July 22, 1865.[57] The ditch was subsequently completed. Ironically, the portion of the ditch that ran through Huffman's land failed several years later, flooding the land of another of Huffman's neighbors, Isaac Mays. In 1873 Greene County installed the "Frick Ditch Alteration," to solve this problem. This project modified a portion of the course of the Frick Ditch, widening that section to fourteen feet and increasing the depth to four and one-half feet.[58]

The construction of the Frick Ditch was made possible by the County Ditch Law, which the Ohio Legislature passed in 1860. It provided "that

the county commissioners of any county shall have power, at any regular session, whenever in their opinion the same is demanded by, or will be conducive to the public health, convenience or welfare, to cause to be established, located and constructed, as herein provided, any ditch, drain or water course within such county." Now the owner of a wetland or flooded land could petition the county commissioners to construct the necessary improvements to drain the land. The landowner had to provide a proposed plan to correct the problem and file a bond, after which the county auditor engaged a surveyor or engineer to lay out the proposed ditch or drain. If approved, all of the landowners affected by the ditch or drain were notified and assessed to pay for the improvements. When sufficient funds were collected, the county would bid out and install the improvements.[59]

In addition to solving the alleged surface drainage problems caused by the Fairfield Mill, the Frick Ditch provided the means to drain the southern section of Huffman Prairie. This was made possible by an innovation that when combined with good ditches could effectively drain wetlands: the clay drain tile. A farmer named John Johnson, of Geneva, New York, sometimes known as "the father of tile drainage in America," introduced this innovation in the United States in 1835. By burying short clay pipes end to end down the middle of his wetlands and fields prone to flooding, Johnson drained away the water that saturated the soil into nearby ditches or streams. The affected fields could then be planted with crops, leading to increased profits. When Johnson started these efforts, in 1839, his neighbors considered him a fanatic, but by 1856 he had proven the utility and profitability of tiling, and his methods subsequently became the standard in the United States for converting wetlands to profitable farmland.[60]

Good drainage was costly: it required that a farmer invest in the labor and materials for ditches and tiles, which might not pay for themselves for several years. However, once these were installed, the farmer was likely to enjoy greatly increased profits. John Klippart's 1861 *Principles and Practice of Land Drainage* discussed at length the theory, history, and methods to achieve good drainage of wetlands. Klippart identified a long list of "objectionable" plant species that can be eliminated by draining. His list would cause any modern-day botanist to shake his or her head, since it included species such as Canada burnet (*Sanguisorba canadensis*), Ohio goldenrod, Riddell's goldenrod, cardinal flower (*Lobelia cardinalis*), showy lady's slipper (*Cypripedium reginae*), and many others that are now rare.

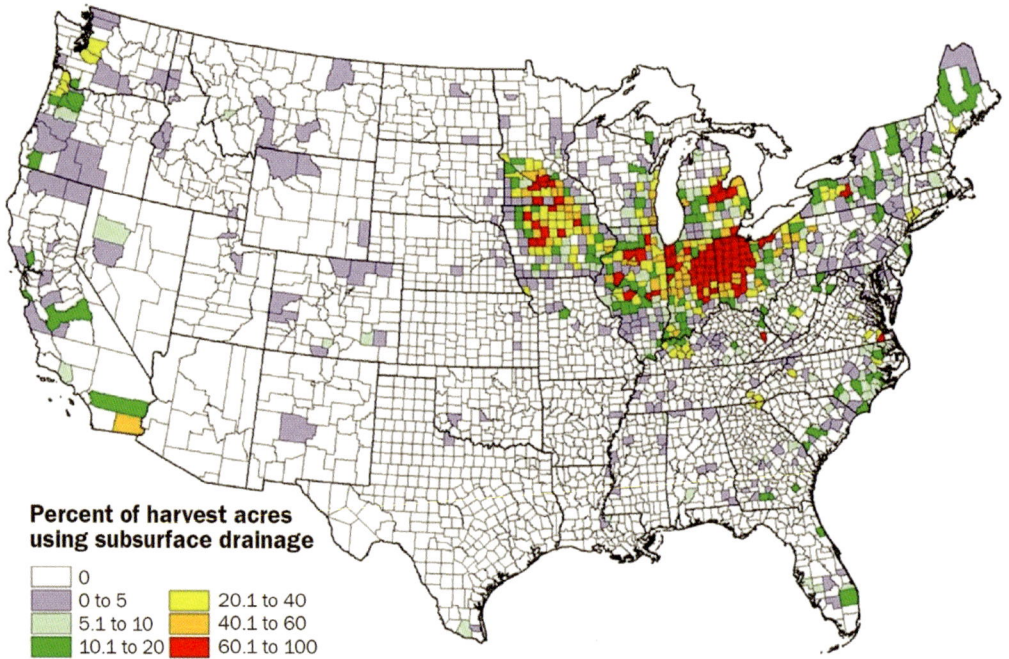

Percent of harvest acres using subsurface drainage

☐ 0	
▧ 0 to 5	▨ 20.1 to 40
▧ 5.1 to 10	▨ 40.1 to 60
▧ 10.1 to 20	▨ 60.1 to 100

Source: 1992 NRI: 1992 Census of Agriculture.

Percent of agricultural land with subsurface drainage in the United States. From 1992 Census of Agriculture.

Annexed is a list of plants whose presence is always an unmistakable evidence of the necessity of drainage—because they flourish only in very moist or wet soil. At the same time, we are well aware that every practical farmer understands the condition of his soil better perhaps than he does botany, but there are others who may wish to engage in agricultural operations who understand botany better than they do the character or condition of soils. . . . As soon as the soil is properly underdrained, all the plants named in the list will disappear, because their accustomed supply of moisture will then be withdrawn, and they, of course, will perish.[61]

This technology subsequently became the standard for farmers in the Midwest, which became one of the most heavily drained regions of the United States; western Ohio's wet prairies, fens, marshes, and swamps were mostly destroyed.[62]

In 1802, Huffman Prairie contained about 750 acres of wet prairie and fen. By 1915, the Huffmans had successfully drained about half of this wetland with an extensive system of ditches and tiles. The portion owned by others to the north of them remained relatively intact, perhaps due

to the excessive labor and expense required to drain it. On the Huffmans'
land, the drained portions of the fen were still frequently wet, and the
peat soil was difficult to work, so the family used these sections for pas-
turing livestock.

In 1904, a piece of this drained fen gained recognition around the
world.

CHAPTER FOUR

The World's First Airfield

On December 15, 1903, Daytonians Orville and Wilbur Wright successfully flew the first powered airplane on the sands of Kitty Hawk, North Carolina.[1] On its best flight, their 1903 Flyer had managed to stay aloft for fifty-nine seconds before landing heavily in the soft sand of the dunes. It was a monumental achievement, but the two inventive brothers were not satisfied: they had yet to achieve sustained or controlled flight. They returned home to Dayton and made plans for the 1904 season. Traveling to the Outer Banks of North Carolina was difficult, so the brothers were determined to find a site closer to Dayton. The best and most practical site they could find was the big field that had been known as Huffman Prairie since the days of John Leonard Riddell's 1834 botany expedition.

The site had several advantages. Perhaps the greatest of these was that it was available. Torrence Huffman, one of William P. Huffman's children, owned the land. A reputable banker in Dayton, he agreed to let the brothers use the eighty-four-acre pasture on his farm for no charge, on condition they drive the livestock out of the field before attempting any flying. He didn't think much of their efforts though, confiding to the farmer who worked the adjacent land for him, "They're fools."[2] The brothers were familiar with the site from bicycle trips they had made to the prairie on the Dayton and Springfield Turnpike with their friend Art Stevens, and Orville may have visited the prairie on a field trip for a high school botany class in 1887.[3] Another advantage of Huffman Prairie was that it was easy to get to from the Wrights' home in Dayton, thanks to the Dayton–Springfield & Urbana Electric Railway

Above: Wright Flyer taking off on Huffman Prairie. Image courtesy of Special Collections and Archives, Wright State University.

Right: Wilbur and Orville Wright at Huffman Prairie in 1904. Image courtesy of Special Collections and Archives, Wright State University.

(DS&U). Also known as a "traction line" or "interurban," the DS&U made its first run from Dayton to Springfield in 1901.[4] The railway served a growing need for quick transportation between population centers, which the turnpikes and railroads built prior to 1900 could not.

Conventional railroads did not run often enough, and travel on the turnpikes was slow and often difficult because they were often in disrepair. The DS&U ran parallel to the Dayton and Springfield Turnpike and crossed Huffman Prairie between the Mad River and Fairfield. It had periodic stops, serviced by wooden platforms, including one called Simms Station, where it crossed the Byron, Yellow Springs, and Clifton Turnpike. With this new transportation system, Orville and Wilbur Wright could easily commute each day from their home in west Dayton.

Wilbur Wright described their chosen flying field to his friend Octave Chanute in a June 21, 1904, letter:

> We are in a large meadow of about 100 acres. It is skirted on the west and north by trees. This not only shuts off the wind somewhat, but gives a slight downward trend. However, this is a matter we do not consider anything serious. The greater troubles are the facts that in addition to the cattle there have been a dozen or more horses in the pasture and as it is surrounded by barbwire fencing we have been at much trouble to get them safely away before making any trials. Also, the ground is an old swamp and is filled with grassy hummocks some six inches high, so that it resembles a prairie dog town.[5]

Wilbur's "hummocks" were likely the remains of fen vegetation. Sedge meadows in the fens of southwestern Ohio are often dominated by a species known as tussock sedge, or *Carex stricta*. These sedges grow from the saturated soil in sturdy clumps. The Frick Ditch and subsequent ditch and tile installations had allowed the Huffmans to

Interurban of the Dayton & Troy line in 1912. Photo courtesy of Special Collections and Archives, Wright State University.

1904 image of Torrence Huffman's pasture on Huffman Prairie, where the Wrights learned to fly in 1904 and 1905. Note the hummocky terrain of the drained fen. Image courtesy of Library of Congress.

Living *Carex stricta* sedge meadow at Siebenthaler Fen in the Beaver Creek Wildlife Area, Beavercreek Township, Greene County, Ohio. This is likely what the Huffman Prairie Flying Field looked like before it was drained.

lower the water table in this part of the fen and wet prairie. Thus, the field was no longer saturated with water to the surface, or it would have been useless as a pasture or flying field. This drainage would be lethal to the sedges, but their sturdy hummocks would take many years to decompose.

That year, the brothers built a shed at the southeast end of the pasture where they could have some privacy and store their aircraft. Their machine had no wheels, so they installed a wooden launch rail on the ground to provide a steady flat surface and minimize friction on takeoff. The hummocky terrain of the drained fen made installation of the launch rail quite difficult, but an even greater problem was a lack of wind. Their craft needed to achieve a speed of twenty-eight miles per hour to become airborne, but it could only reach twenty-four miles per hour on its own on the rail. Every time the brothers flew, they had to install the track so as to face the expected winds, which provided additional lift. In September 1904, they solved this problem with the installation of a catapult launch system that utilized a tower, heavy weight, ropes, and pulleys to give the plane a boost. This greatly increased their success, and by the end of the year they made their first full turns in the air.[6] In 1905, they built a slightly larger shed to the north of the 1904 structure. By the end of that year, their 1905 Flyer stayed aloft for over thirty-nine minutes and circled the field nearly thirty times on a single flight.[7] The brothers had created the world's first manned, practical airplane.

The achievements in 1904 and 1905 at Huffman Prairie were the product of years of insightful thinking, research, and experimentation. The Wrights had deduced that a pilot needed to control an aircraft in three dimensions: pitch (the movement of the nose up and down), yaw (the nose turning right and left), and roll (each wingtip moving up or down). The biggest challenge was roll, and Wilbur Wright determined how to achieve this motion in an airplane by watching birds. He noted how they adjusted their flights by changing the angle of their wings. One day in 1899, while pondering in the bicycle shop how to mimic the avian technique, he started twisting a cardboard inner tube box. Then the thought occurred to him that an aircraft's wings could be twisted in flight with wire to produce and control roll, an innovation known as "wing-warping."[8]

Between 1904 and 1916, Huffman Prairie was the subject of a rich inventory of photographs. While most of these photos were produced to document aviation, they also provide a good record of land use in and adjacent to the flying field. These pictures indicate that the Huffman Prairie Flying Field pasture was mostly bordered by crop fields between 1904 and 1911. The exception was the large unfarmed field to the north and northwest, which continued to harbor wet prairie and fen habitat.

One account of the Wrights' activities included an adventure in the undrained portion of the prairie. Written by *Dayton Daily News* writer Roz Young, it tells a story of the Stevens family, friends of Orville and Wilbur.

Open ditch on boundary of flying field on Huffman Prairie. The aircraft is a Wright Model-A Flyer. Ditches and tiles in a drained wetland must be maintained continually to keep the soil from being saturated with water. Image courtesy of Special Collections and Archives, Wright State University.

Above: Wright Model B Flyer in front of 1910 hangar. Photo taken from the Byron, Yellow Springs, & Clifton Turnpike, looking southeast. Note the field in the background that is in tall crops, probably corn. Image courtesy of Special Collections and Archives, Wright State University.

Right: Wilbur and Orville at Huffman Prairie in 1904. Photographer facing southwest. The large field beyond the pasture is in corn. Note the pastured look of the vegetation, closely cropped grass studded with inedible plants such as ironweed. Image courtesy of Library of Congress.

Mrs. Stevens often packed picnic baskets, and they drove in the family buggy to Huffman Prairie on Saturday afternoons to watch the brothers fly. They were joined by other Daytonians and, in Helen's words, "They never flew very high, and the frequent, unexpected landings caused great excitement and merriment to the many observers beside the road. A concerned farm woman nearby kept a bucket of water, rag bandages and salve for any injuries that might occur to the flyers. Her small son would take off, bucket in hand, to the crash site, thoroughly enjoying his mission.

"One day, as my father and his hired man were driving cattle to the stockyards, a high-spirited young bull suddenly broke away and headed across the prairie. The stretch was notorious for pockets of quicksand and rattlesnakes—definitely a nasty place to chase a bull. He had not

gone far when he stumbled into a pool of quicksand and started thrashing around violently. When the two men saw there was no way for them to pull the bull out, my father raced across to the Wright hangar. He explained their predicament to Orville Wright, who hurried out to a recently purchased tractor, grabbed ropes and planks and drove to the terrified beast. After much tugging and pulling, the bull was oozed out. All involved were exhausted as well as very slimy."⁹

The brothers ceased activities on the prairie for several years while they pursued patents and demonstrated their machine in Europe and elsewhere in the United States. They returned in 1910, when they built a new and larger hangar near Simms Station. Here, they operated a

Aerial photo taken in 1911, photographer facing northwest. This photo shows the 1910 hangar used for the Wright Flying School, just to the south of the Byron, Yellow Springs & Clifton Turnpike. Also visible is the wood platform for the Simms Station Dayton–Springfield & Urbana Electric Railway stop. Note the large open wet prairie still unfarmed in the background. Image courtesy of Special Collections and Archives, Wright State University.

flying school with their new Wright Company, where 119 pilots earned their wings.[10] The school was short-lived; Wilbur died in 1912, and Orville sold the company in 1915.[11] However, the Wrights' monumental achievements would have a lasting impact on aviation history, the Dayton area, and the big prairie first documented by Benjamin Van Cleve.

CHAPTER FIVE

From Floodplain to Air Force Base

In late March 1913, a storm of unprecedented proportions swept through the valley of the Great Miami River (Miami Valley). From March 23 to March 27, between nine and eleven inches of rain fell. Existing levees were overrun, and most of the valley's cities received major flooding. The flood crested on the twenty-sixth, at ten feet in downtown Dayton. As many as 123 people died in the Dayton area, at least 1,000 homes were destroyed, and some 1,500 horses drowned. There were also tremendous losses of life and property in other communities, particularly Hamilton, Middletown, and Piqua.[1]

The leaders and citizens of the Miami Valley were determined to prevent a flood like this from happening again. The Miami Conservancy District (MCD) was formed in June 1915 to design, build, and manage a flood control system for the region. The district hired engineer Arthur E. Morgan to lead the effort. Morgan and his staff envisioned a series of five dams on the major rivers of the valley, strategically located to take advantage of local geology and provide maximum protection. The dams were designed to be dry; they would impound water from a flood but would release it all back into the river over time. However, to do this the district had to own the land on which the dams would be built and have the legal right to back up floodwaters behind the dams. To accomplish this, the district used its power of eminent domain. Each parcel of land was appraised and the owners offered fair market value, with a total cost of the land and improvements estimated at $34 million. MCD borrowed these funds, secured by bonds, which were a lien on the estimated benefits that the improvements would realize. The bonds were retired by an increase in property taxes for the landowners who

Above: Flooding in downtown Dayton in March 1913. From Miami Conservancy District Records. Image courtesy of Special Collections and Archives, Wright State University.

Right: Huffman Dam as completed in 1922. Image courtesy of the Miami Conservancy District.

benefited from the flood control improvements; they were fully retired in 1949.[2]

The Huffman Dam, on the Mad River east of Dayton, was one of the five created by MCD. It was built just west of the presettlement Huffman Prairie, which in 1915 was part of twenty prosperous farms. Its construction was a massive undertaking: the completed dam was 65 feet high and contained 1.67 million cubic yards of earth. MCD called the land that could be flooded by each dam a "retarding basin." If the Huffman Dam retarding basin was filled to capacity, it would store 124,000 acre-feet of water, about 40 billion gallons, and create a 7,300-acre lake.[3]

Another massive project MCD had to complete was the rerouting of the existing roads, railroads, and electric trolley around the retarding basin. To accomplish this, it made a cut into the limestone bedrock southwest of Huffman Prairie to obtain a new alignment that would not be flooded, should the dam back up water. Another item that had to be moved was the village of Osborn, just north of Huffman Prairie. This entire town was moved to a new location east of the village of Fairfield. In 1950, the two combined and became the city of Fairborn.[4]

By 1922, all of the land that had comprised the presettlement prairie and fen complex had passed from private ownership to MCD ownership. However, the district did not intend to keep this land; its board planned to place an easement on each tract it purchased. These easements would give MCD the right to back floodwater onto the properties and forbid building new habitable structures or bringing in fill material that would

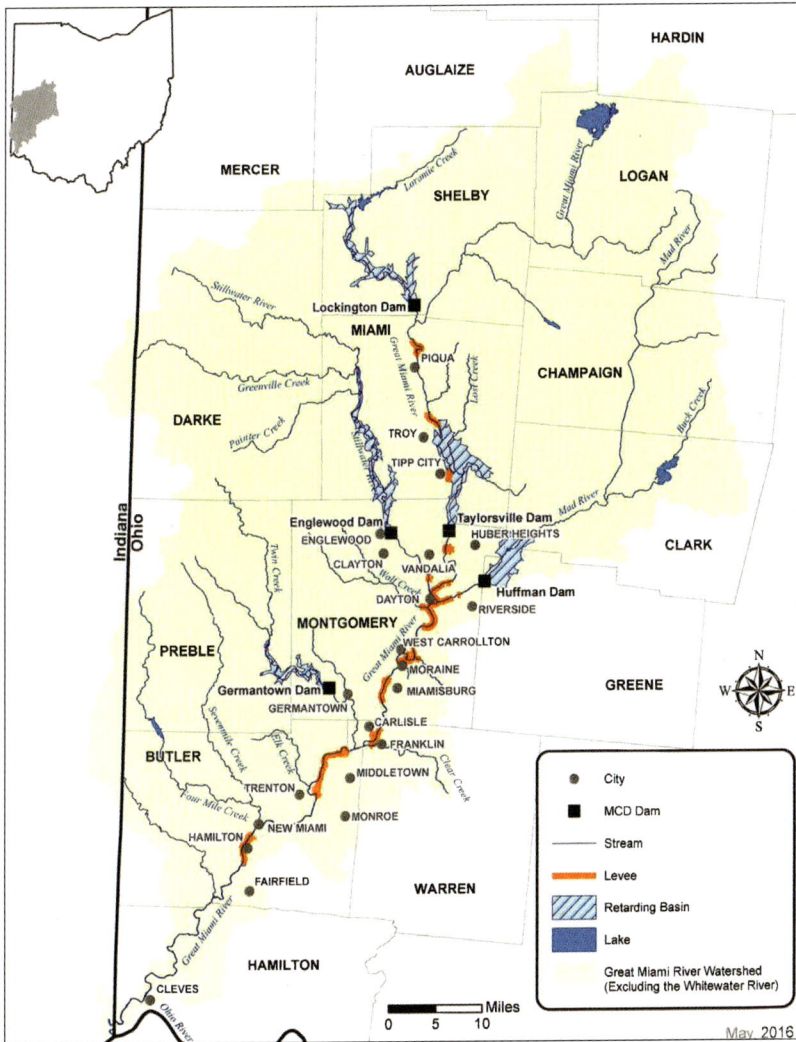

The Miami Conservancy District Flood Prevention System. Image courtesy of the Miami Conservancy District.

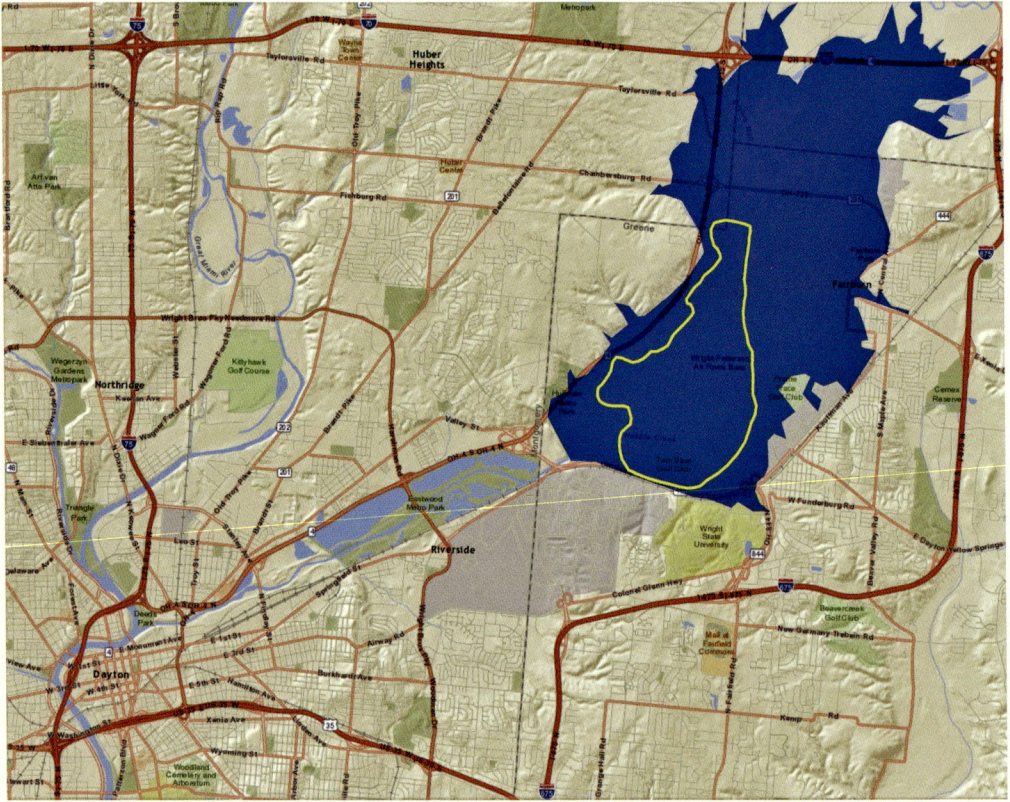

Above: Retarding basin of Huffman Dam. The area in blue would be covered by floodwater when the dam is at maximum capacity. The area outlined in yellow is the presettlement Huffman Prairie.

Photo taken from what is now the Wright Memorial, looking northeast, in January 1922. The foreground shows the cut made for the relocation of the Big Four Railroad line. The background shows Huffman Prairie and the abandoned Dayton & Springfield Turnpike. Image courtesy of the Miami Conservancy District.

Job 5-2849A

take up space that could otherwise hold floodwater. It would sell the
land back to private landowners with no other restrictions.[5]

After the Wright brothers' achievements at Huffman Prairie, the federal
government slowly began to realize aviation's importance and potential.
In August 1916, Congress appropriated almost $13.9 million for military
aviation and added a supplemental appropriation of $600,000 for the
purchase of land to use as flying fields and depots.[6] The government then
started a search for suitable sites. Dayton engineer and industrialist
Edward Deeds was also one of the founders of the Miami Conservancy
District. He was determined to establish a field in the Dayton area. He
knew that the Huffman retarding basin upstream from the proposed
Huffman Dam was in the process of being purchased by the MCD and
lobbied for this site to be chosen for a new government flying field.

Deeds and the local community were successful in their lobbying
efforts. In May 1917, the MCD leased 2,075 acres of the Huffman retarding basin to the U.S. Army, including the Wright brothers' old flying
field and most of the presettlement Huffman Prairie, to establish Wilbur
Wright Field. The army immediately marshaled extensive labor and
material to build the field, centered west of the village of Fairfield. New
structures were built on land slightly higher than the rest of the lease
area, including a string of twelve 120-by-66-foot aviation hangars.[7] By
the end of July 1917, over eight hundred personnel were stationed at
the field. There were no runways; aircraft merely landed and took off
from the open grassy field.

"MAKING READY" U.S. AVIA

Above: The construction of Wilbur Wright Field on June 9, 1917, just west of Fairfield, Ohio. The presettlement Huffman Prairie, now largely converted to farms, lies in the background. Image courtesy of Library of Congress.

Right: Wilbur Wright Field between 1924 and 1927. Image courtesy of Wright-Patterson Air Force Base archives.

MISC. 86. FAIRFIELD OHIO.

The airfield had drainage problems from the start. When the army took possession in 1917, it changed the ditch system to go around the proposed flying field. The reconfigured drainage system the army had installed was insufficient to carry off storm water from the Fairfield Mill tailrace (Hebble Creek). This ditch would easily overtop its banks after a storm, making portions of the field unusable for aircraft. The same waters that had confounded Jacob Frick now stymied the U.S. Army.

In May 1918, Major Arthur E. Wilbourn, Wilbur Wright Field's commanding officer, submitted to Washington the first annual report on the condition of the new field. The flooding was especially concerning to him, and he bluntly blamed the problem on a combination of poor construction work and undrainable topography:

> The land between the main drainage ditch and the Mad River, which consists of the low, bottom-land referred to above, is used as the Flying Field. Efforts were made by the Construction Division to grade this land. This work was done in a highly unsatisfactory way. In the first place, the draining of such an area is quite difficult from an engineering standpoint, when consideration is given to the fact that some places of

FAIRFIELD, O. JUNE 9TH, 1917.

Flooding of Wilbur Wright Field in 1917. Image courtesy of Wright-Patterson Air Force Base archives.

the field are approximately on a level with the river. . . . There are many small depressions. After each rain these depressions are filled with water. It is impossible for these pools to be drained in any direction, since the river level is so near the level of the field. A sub-soil drainage system would probably act so as to efficiently flood the field whenever the water in the river was slightly above normal.[8]

Arthur Morgan, chief engineer of the MCD, assessed the problem. He visited the site and discussed the matter with Major Wilbourn. Morgan blamed the army for the flooding: it had filled in existing ditches and

Damaged biplane on Wilbur Wright Field in 1918. Note the bare gravel exposed by efforts to level the field. Photo courtesy of Library of Congress.

constructed a drainage channel one-fifth of the size necessary to handle the storm water. He maintained that the field was twenty-three feet above the level of the Mad River, and drainage of surface waters should not be a problem. Indeed, the previous landowners and Greene County had solved this problem over fifty years earlier. When the issue became one of public debate, Morgan spoke about it in an interview with the *Dayton Daily News* on September 15, 1918, bluntly refuting Wilbourn's assessment of the problem:

> The difficulty, which has been experienced there, has been due to the fact that the army officers in charge of the field were too burdened with other work to give it attention or were unfamiliar with such drainage problems and did not handle them intelligently. . . . Not only did Major Wilbourne fail to carry out the simple and necessary work for draining the field, but he made a report to Washington to the effect that the field could not be drained by ordinary means. . . . Except for a low wet tract along the Big Four railroad, which comprises fifteen or twenty per cent of the whole field, the Wright field is admirably situated for perfect drainage.[9]

The "low wet tract" Morgan referred to would indicate that in 1918 between 240 and 320 acres of Huffman Prairie's original wet prairie/fen complex remained on the 1,600 acres of floodplain land on Wilbur Wright Field.

Another issue for Wilbur Wright Field was its somewhat uneven surface on the east end. The field had small knolls that could be problematic for pilots and resulted in many accidents. The army's solution was to grade off the high spots, fill in the low spots, and replant bare spots with purchased grass seed. This work left large areas of bare gravel that were unable to grow thick grass.[10]

One early improvement installed at Wilbur Wright Field that had an impact on the prairie was the speed course, a two-mile course laid out on the prairie to test new aircraft. It was marked so it could be easily seen and followed from a speeding airplane. This course was the subject of a 1929 *Popular Mechanics* article.

> The first flight step in this system for a new plane, after a pilot has given it preliminary runs to get thoroughly the "feel" of his ship, is taking it over the "speed course." This is a two-mile straightaway, permanently laid out on the test field, set off by markers and with a long black line down the middle. These tests require more expert piloting than any others flown, for in order that he may safely see the markers, and fly directly in line with the black line, holding his plane at an even level, where the air is quietest, the speed course is flown low—a mere ten to twenty feet off the ground. A calm day is always chosen. Braced steadily in his seat behind the windshield, tense against any slightest movement, with one hand the pilot grasps the control stick, with the other, the engine throttle, with a stop watch in one of the hands is held from slipping by having the

Plane flying low over Wilbur Wright Field in 1924. Photo by William Preston Mayfield, courtesy of Dayton History.

Wilbur Wright Field map showing speed course. Image courtesy of Wright-Patterson Air Force Base archives.

cord wrapped between the fingers. No chance of escape by parachute should anything go wrong. The pilot could only land, hurtling at the ground, and probably crash.[11]

Wilbur Wright Field was discontinued as a pilot training field after World War I. The army's aviation engineering and testing facility at Mc-Cook Field, in Dayton, was also to be closed, mainly because that field was too small. The government intended to build a new base for aviation engineering purposes somewhere but was asking local communities to donate the necessary land. Local business leaders were concerned about the loss to the local economy and the departure of aviation from the place where it all started. The Dayton Air Service Committee was formed in 1922 to raise funds to purchase lands for a new facility. This group identified a land base totaling 4,998 acres, most of which was Wilbur Wright Field, still owned by the MCD; the balance was in seven privately owned farms. The committee quickly raised $425,673 to acquire the land.[12]

The rich farms on Huffman Prairie that the MCD had purchased and the army had partly converted to Wilbur Wright Field now contained abandoned buildings and building foundations, roads, large areas of bare gravel, and a drainage system that had been abandoned or changed to suit an airfield. Maintaining ditches and drain tiles in the wetter portions away from the active airfield was not a priority for the army as it had been for the former landowners. Without maintenance, the ditch and tile systems had begun to break down, and formerly drained fields started to become wet again. Also in 1922, a significant acreage of undrained, original wet prairie and fen remained in the western side of the field. MCD farm manager S. Graham Smith documented these conditions, none of which were perceived as good, in a letter to Ezra M. Kuhns, the MCD secretary-treasurer, on November 27, 1922:

> There are several hundred acres of this area which are at present worth-less for any agricultural purpose, due to lack of drainage. There are other hundreds of acres, (area unknown but much more that the first class mentioned), which have some value for pasture but are not tillable on account of insufficient drainage and the peaty nature of the soil. Due to the gradual, natural filling of the few ditches now remaining, the area of both these classes is increasing from year to year. In preparing the land for a flying field during this time some 2250 acres of the area were under lease to the United States Government many ditches were filled and knolls and higher ridges lowered. As the subsoil under these high spots consisted of a rather coarse, fairly clean gravel and as the soil and some of the subsoil was scraped off and deposited in the lower places, the result has been that not only are these original knoll locations left practically sterile, but so also is some of the land on which this coarse gravel was deposited.
>
> The land on which the Government erected buildings during the time of its lease now vacated and with buildings removed, as well as that part of the tract still under lease on which buildings are now stand-ing, has been rendered almost valueless for agriculture by the large concrete floors and foundations, the cost of removal of which would in many places exceed the market value of the land after cleaning.[13]

Abandoned hangar on Wilbur Wright Field. Image courtesy of the Miami Conservancy District.

At the end of the letter, Smith recommended that the board accept the offer of $75,000 from the Dayton Air Service Committee for the purchase of 3,853 acres of MCD land. MCD approved the sale but retained a flood easement on the entire acreage, which was its main reason for purchasing it in the first place.[14] On August 9, 1924, the Air Service Committee

Above: Spectators at the 1924 International Air Races at Wilbur Wright Field. Photo by William Preston Mayfield. Image courtesy of Dayton History.

Right: Lieutenant H. H. Mills, winner of the Pulitzer trophy at the 1924 International Air Races. Mills won the race in a Verville Sperry. Image courtesy of Wright-Patterson Air Force Base archives.

donated 4,520 acres, including the entire original Huffman Prairie, to the U.S. government.[15]

October 2–4, 1924, Wilbur Wright Field hosted the International Air Races. Dayton schools as well as city and county offices closed on the Friday of the event. A Friday-evening banquet at the National Cash Register Company (NCR) dining hall, hosted by the National Aeronautic Association, had a thousand participants. Over a hundred thousand spectators attended the event, watching the show from a grandstand that was over a mile long.[16] The event's most prestigious prize was the Pulitzer Trophy, awarded for the fastest time over a closed course. Lieutenant H. H. Mills won that race, with an average speed of 216.55 mph. Not so fortunate was Captain Burt E. Skeel, a popular U.S. Army pilot who lost his life during the race for the Pulitzer, when he was diving in his Curtis R-6 Racer to gain speed to start the race.

Spectators saw Skeel's R-6 hurtling downward in a 60-degree dive. . . . The loudspeakers blared, "Here comes Skeel. Note his speed." About a mile and a half from the starting point . . . a sudden swerve of his plane showed something was wrong. Sunlight flashed on what looked like "a bursting shell" as the cooling water burst from the ruptured wing radiators, sprayed out, and refracted the sunlight. . . . The fuselage, part of the lower wing still attached, hit the earth nearly vertically, at the tremendous speed built from the dive and buried itself in the swampy earth, disappearing from view. Several hours passed before the fuselage was found, and even more before Captain Skeel's body was located at

Above: Mock-up of New York City constructed on Wilbur Wright Field for the 1924 International Air Races. Image courtesy of Wright-Patterson Air Force Base archives.

Right: Mock-up of New York City being destroyed by aerial bombing at the conclusion of the 1924 International Air Races. Image from *Popular Science Monthly,* January 1925.

a depth variously reported as 10 and 14 feet . . . The apparent explosion, the plunging airplane, the inevitability of the crash, the geyser of earth and debris thrown up at impact stilled the 50,000 spectators except for gasps and moans.[17]

Wright-Patterson Air Force Base later named Skeel Avenue after this daring pilot whose life was ended on Huffman Prairie.

The air race concluded with perhaps the most bizarre event ever to occur on Huffman Prairie: the aerial bombing of a mock-up of New York

City. A large replica of the Big Apple, containing over fifty wooden structures, was built in the middle of the field. The replica of the Woolworth Building was over one hundred feet tall. The fake city was the target of aircraft that dropped live bombs to demonstrate the "tactics, accuracy, and power of aerial bombardment." A subsequent article and drawing in *Popular Science Monthly* described the event: "The destruction of a model City of New York in 30 minutes by air raiders was the startling spectacle that closed the recent International Air Races at Dayton, Ohio. This Illustration shows the aerial bombs bursting among the city's skyscrapers and in the air the exploding shells from anti-aircraft guns. The spectacle was staged as a demonstration of the deadly effectiveness of aircraft as weapons of modern warfare, and imagination supplies the horrors."[18]

This simulated bombing of New York City at the 1924 International Air Races took place at a time when there was a major debate within the armed forces about what to prioritize and fund. Colonel Billy Mitchell, a successful leader of the American aerial units in Europe in World War I, was a frequent visitor to Wilbur Wright Field in the early 1920s.[19] After the war, he was convinced the airplane should replace the navy as America's first line of defense and that a strategic bomber force should be developed with the capability to hit an enemy behind the lines.[20] In 1921 he successfully demonstrated that big, expensive battleships were obsolete. Mitchell's bomber force successfully sank several obsolete warships, including two battleships, with bombs dropped from aircraft. However, his beliefs and ego did not endear him to traditionalists in the U.S. military. His rhetoric became increasingly heated, and in 1925 he wrote of the "incompetency, criminal negligence, and the almost treasonable negligence of our national defense by the War and Navy departments."[21] For this he was subsequently court-martialed, and he resigned from the army in 1926. During World War II, his ideas that air power could sink battleships and inflict damage on industrial cities were proved correct.

In 1925, all of the land that the Dayton Air Service Committee had donated to the federal government was renamed Wright Field. In 1931, the portion containing the former Wilbur Wright Field and the pre-settlement prairie were named Patterson Field, in honor of Lieutenant Frank Stuart Patterson, who was killed there when his plane crashed in 1918.[22] Patterson was the son of Frank J. Patterson, who with his brother John H. Patterson had founded NCR in 1884.

As aviation technology advanced through the 1930s, aircraft became increasingly heavy and could no longer use open grass fields for daily

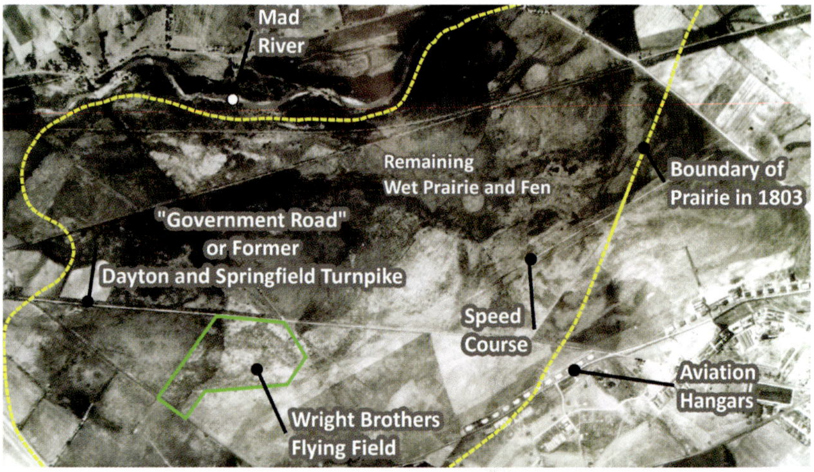
Mad
River
Remaining
Wet Prairie and Fen
Boundary of
Prairie in 1803
"Government Road"
or Former
Dayton and Springfield Turnpike
Speed
Course
Aviation
Hangars
Wright Brothers
Flying Field

Patterson Field in 1930. Most of the land west of the speed course was not actively managed. Note the large area of wet prairie still present. Image courtesy of Wright-Patterson Air Force Base archives.

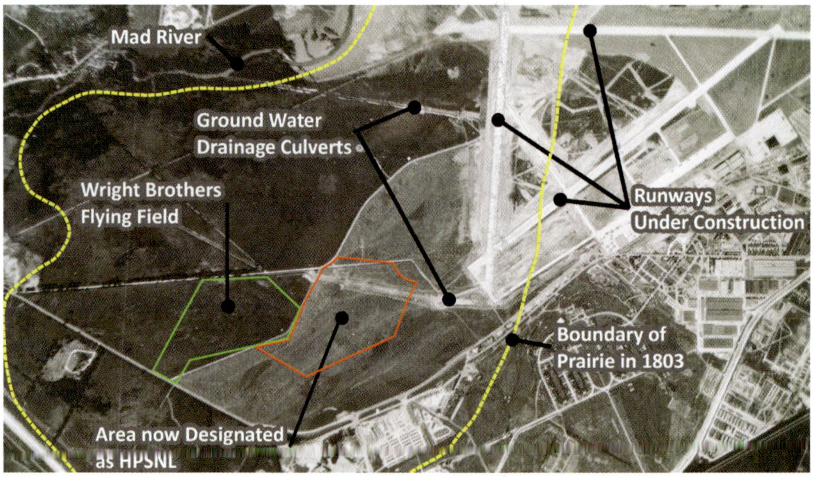
Mad River
Ground Water
Drainage Culverts
Wright Brothers
Flying Field
Runways
Under Construction
Boundary of
Prairie in 1803
Area now Designated
as HPSNL

Patterson field in 1942, with three new concrete runways under construction. Note the newly installed drainage culverts diverting groundwater to the Mad River.

Interior of runway drainage culvert in 2016, carrying strong flow of groundwater.

Construction of Very Heavy Bomber runway on Patterson Field in 1947. Image courtesy of Wright-Patterson Air Force Base archives.

operations. The solution was the construction of concrete runways, built on Patterson Field between 1942 and 1956. These projects required extensive drainage systems to carry away the abundant groundwater under and near the runways. These runways and their drainage systems were a vital upgrade to military aviation on the field but also caused the destruction of the remaining wet prairie and fen habitat.

The first project, which the Army Air Corps installed in 1942 and 1943, was the construction of three large concrete runways and taxiways arranged in a triangular pattern.[23] To keep the runways dry, large underground concrete pipes (still functioning today) conveyed the groundwater to the southwest, where they emptied into a large ditch, dubbed Trout Creek, that carried the water to the Mad River.

In 1947, the Army Air Corps became its own branch of the military, the U.S. Air Force. That year, a new and larger runway, the Very Heavy Bomber runway, was installed on Patterson Field; this was extended in 1956.[24] This project also installed a major drainage system. When built,

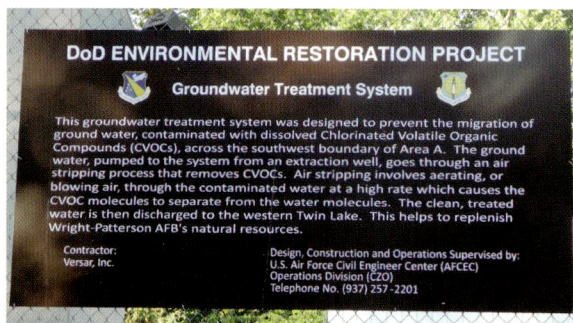

Above: Sign explaining remediation of groundwater pollution on WPAFB, 2016.

Right: Air stripping tower, used to remove volatile organic compounds from contaminated groundwater.

this big runway was eight thousand feet long and three hundred feet wide. It was intended to accommodate the new large bombers and jet-powered aircraft. Between 1963 and 1975, the big runway was used by B-52 bombers of the 17th Bombardment Wing and KC-135 refueling tankers of the 922d Air Refueling Squadron. These aircraft had a nuclear deterrent mission, but they also supplied aircraft and aircrews for the war in Southeast Asia.[25]

In January 1948, Patterson Field and the nearby Wright Field became components of the newly designated Wright-Patterson Air Force Base (WPAFB).

World War II and the Cold War era greatly expanded industrial shops and research and development laboratories on WPAFB, which generated waste products that required disposal. Between 1941 and 1973, several unlined waste disposal landfills, four of which were on the presettlement Huffman Prairie, were created throughout the base to dispose of this material. Materials landfilled included some 791 tons of waste—solvents, contaminated thinners, degreasing sludges, tetraethyllead sludge, and miscellaneous hazardous chemicals.[26] Unfortunately, these chemicals found their way into the groundwater below the landfills and threatened the safety of nearby wells used by WPAFB and the City of Dayton. WPAFB and the Ohio Environmental Protection Agency identified the extent of

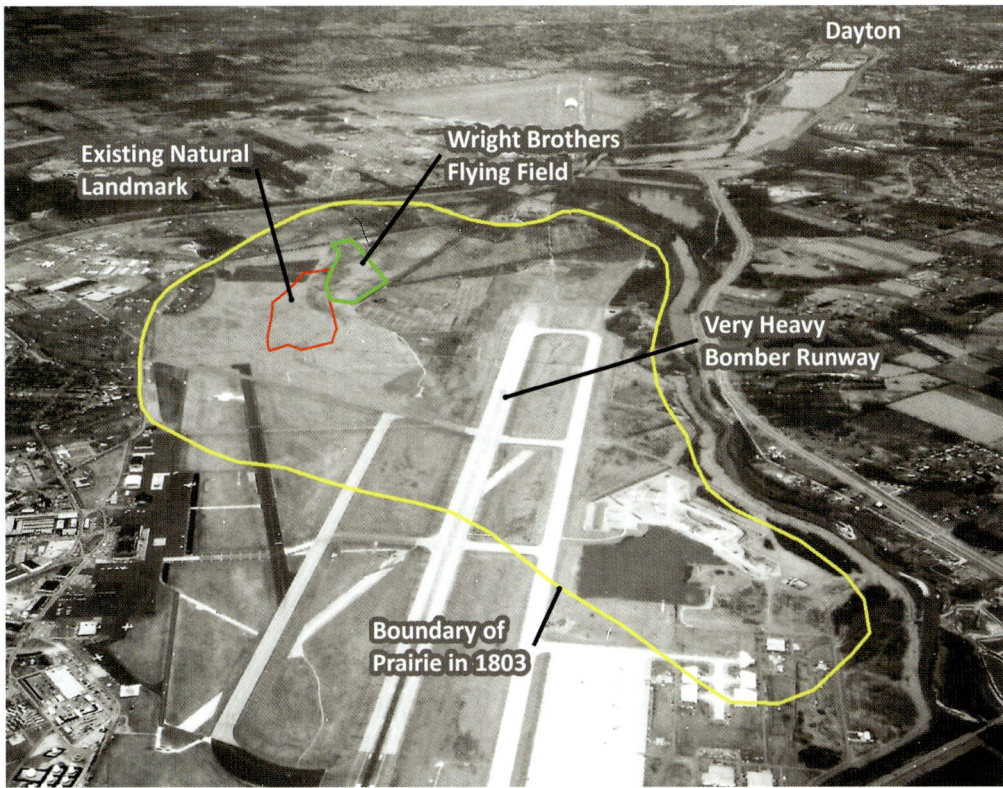

Labels on image:
- Dayton
- Existing Natural Landmark
- Wright Brothers Flying Field
- Very Heavy Bomber Runway
- Boundary of Prairie in 1803

Patterson field circa 1970. Note that nearly all of the presettlement Huffman Prairie is developed or mowed. Photo from author's collection.

the problem in 1985, and since that time these former landfills have been the focus of a major cleanup and remediation effort.[27]

Since the formation of Wright-Patterson Air Force Base in 1948, there has been limited development of the land south of the Very Heavy Bomber runway on Patterson Field, and the land has largely remained open space. The Twin Base golf course was built on the south end in 1963 and a skeet shooting range just east of the Wright Brothers flying field in the mid-1960s. "Food strips" were sometimes planted; these grain crops, including corn, sorghum, sunflowers, millet, and milo, encouraged small game. Other fields were leased to farmers to grow crops or cut hay.[28] Since 1951, a portion of this open land has been managed as a shooting preserve for WPAFB personnel. Each fall, a series of access strips is mowed to create lanes for hunters to walk through and hunt rabbits and released pheasants.[29] In addition to these recreational management actions, much of the land was mowed several times per year in the growing season to keep it free of tall or woody vegetation.[30]

By the 1970s, all of the changes to the land since Israel Ludlow's time had eliminated all visible traces of the complex prairie and fen habitat

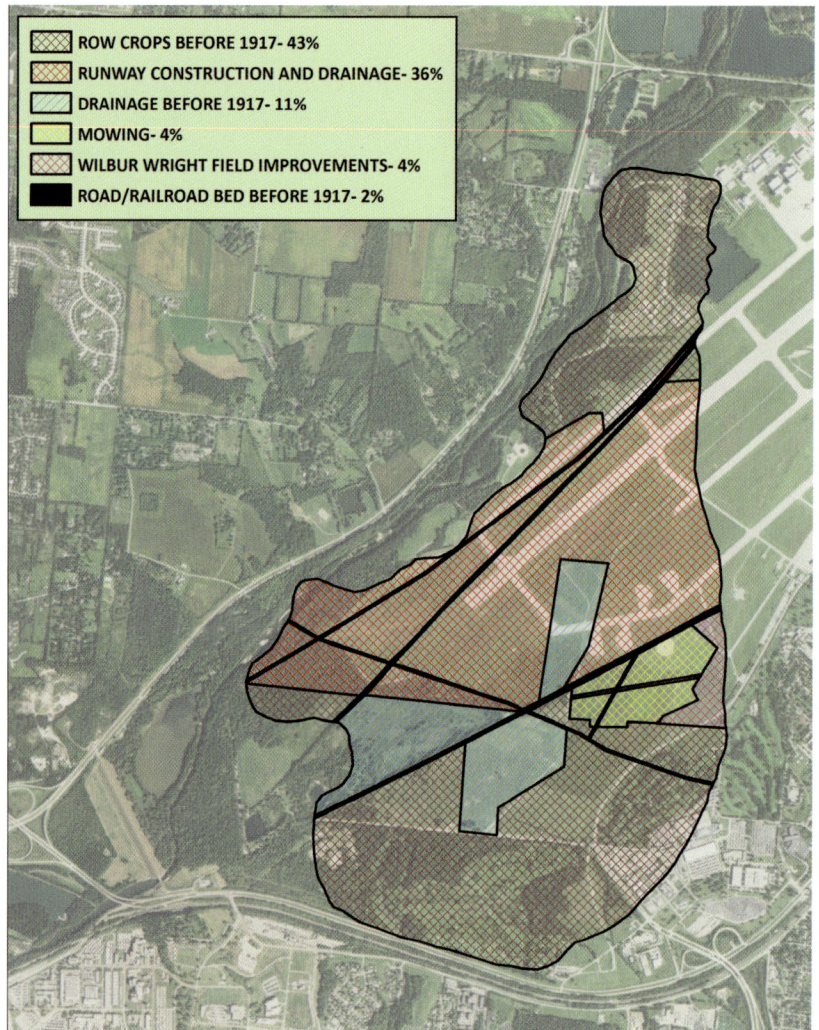

Factors contributing to loss of prairie habitat at Huffman Prairie.

Legend:
- ROW CROPS BEFORE 1917- 43%
- RUNWAY CONSTRUCTION AND DRAINAGE- 36%
- DRAINAGE BEFORE 1917- 11%
- MOWING- 4%
- WILBUR WRIGHT FIELD IMPROVEMENTS- 4%
- ROAD/RAILROAD BED BEFORE 1917- 2%

that had thrived there for thousands of years. The prairie and fen had been lost to four major agents of change:

1. About 56 percent of the original prairie was destroyed or severely degraded by farming, agricultural drainage, and installation of roads and railroads prior to 1917.
2. About 4 percent was destroyed or severely degraded by the work done to improve and maintain Wilbur Wright Field between 1917 and 1919.
3. About 36 percent, including most of the remaining wet prairie and fen, was destroyed by the installation of large modern runways and their corresponding drainage systems between 1942 and 1956.
4. Any remaining prairie vegetation was mowed on a regular rotation through the growing season as part of base maintenance protocol.

The big prairie was gone, but the human and American achievements on this grassland in less than eighty years were unprecedented. Here the first practical powered aircraft had been tested and flown, with a large impact on world history. The prairie was an important part of an innovative flood-control system that has protected Dayton and other communities along the Great Miami River from flooding. Here the Wright Company School of Aviation trained the world's first generation of pilots. The prairie land became an important part of Wright-Patterson Air Force base, an important facility for national defense. Wright-Patt supports world-class aviation, engineering, and research facilities and is a major employer for the region.

That these achievements resulted in the loss of the biologically diverse living systems that once thrived on the landscape was not widely known or considered except by a few. Agnes Anderson Hall, John Van Cleve's biographer, reflected on the progress and loss at Huffman Prairie in "Letters from John":

> The "wet prairie" has lost its fringed gentians, in deed, but in the first years of this century its flat expanse recommended itself to two young men of the Van Cleve blood and tradition—as a place well adapted to experiments with their new invention—a machine that would fly! A Government Flying Field now bears their name on the spot where one day a breathless crowd watched in tense silence while Orville Wright soared three thousand feet into the air! The Wright brothers led the way into the wilderness of the air as the Van Cleves had ventured forth on earth; they scaled the ramparts of the clouds as those, their forbears, had scaled the Alleghenies; they faced the scorn of unbelief, and beat back dangers and possessed their goal with the same courage, the same indomitable perseverance, the same effacement of self. Their lives were as full of peril and daring; their deeds were as replete with romance.[31]

Environmental awareness and general understanding of the complexity and value of living systems were a science and ethic that didn't start in a meaningful way until the early twentieth century, but they grew swiftly in the 1970s and 1980s. This increased awareness and valuation of biodiversity and natural systems was to combine with a bit of luck to bring back a piece of Huffman Prairie in 1986.

CHAPTER SIX

A Prairie Renaissance

In 1800, the prairies of Ohio covered about 2.5 percent of the state and 17 percent of Bath Township in northwest Greene County.[1] By the 1950s, the complex plant and animal communities had been reduced to a few scattered and forgotten fragments in the back of private land parcels, thin strips along a few railroad rights-of-way, and a few pioneer cemeteries.

The first significant effort to reestablish prairie vegetation in Ohio was started at the Aullwood Audubon Center and Farm north of Dayton, in 1959.[2] Center staff decided to create a prairie in an abandoned crop field to provide an opportunity to teach children and adults about this lost ecosystem. They collected seed from remnant prairies in Adams County and hand-planted them in a one-acre plot of plowed soil near the nature center. Results were mixed, but the determined naturalists gradually expanded their efforts, going as far as western Indiana to find enough seed to continue the project. They added new plots most years through 1972 and tried different methods. Seeds from at least seventy-four species of prairie plants were harvested from prairie remnants and hand-planted on-site. Over time, the former old field was transformed into a lush, ten-acre re-creation of a mesic prairie. The Aullwood prairie educated and inspired large numbers of children and adults and created a regional interest in a forgotten subject.

On October 23, 1971, T. Richard Fisher of Bowling Green State University called a meeting at the Aullwood Audubon Center to discuss what could be done to protect the few remaining natural prairies of Ohio. This seed germinated in 1974, when Charles C. King, director of the Ohio Biological Survey, proposed a formal inventory of the state's remaining

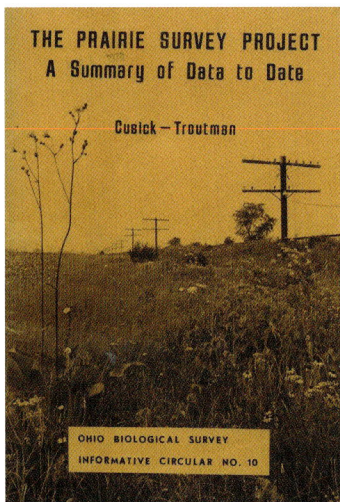

THE PRAIRIE SURVEY PROJECT
A Summary of Data to Date

Cusick — Troutman

OHIO BIOLOGICAL SURVEY
INFORMATIVE CIRCULAR NO. 10

Cover of booklet summarizing the results of the Ohio prairie survey project, published by the Ohio Biological Survey in 1978.

prairies to the board of that organization. The board approved the creation of the Ohio Prairie Survey Project and charged it to "identify areas of existing prairie and prairie species in Ohio."[3] Prairie enthusiast K. Roger Troutman served as the chairman of the project and state botanist Allison W. Cusick as data coordinator. About sixty-five volunteer researchers then scoured the countryside looking for remnant prairies, each of which was carefully documented and its status ascertained. The Ohio Biological Survey published the initial results in 1978. This small yellow booklet reached many people, significantly increased awareness of Ohio's prairies, and initiated several efforts to protect remaining sites. Through the 1980s and 1990s, thanks to the Prairie Survey Project, many people caught prairie fever and became prairie enthusiasts. The Ohio Prairie Association was formed in 1999.[4]

This author was one of many who caught the fever. While working at an internship for the Park District of Dayton-Montgomery County in 1981, I was introduced to the prairie inventory project and the agency's early efforts to plant prairie vegetation on parkland. In 1982, I entered graduate school at Wright State University to study biology and find a way to make a living doing habitat management work. During that time, my advisor, James Runkle, was studying Israel Ludlow's 1802–3 survey notes to gather information on the presettlement forests of Bath Township, particularly the mature woods on the campus.

I was fascinated by these notes and maps and noticed that the references to prairies in the surveyor's field notes corresponded to irregular shapes marked by dotted lines on the surveyor's plat maps. With these as a guide, I scoured back corners of farms in Bath Township where Ludlow had found these prairies. In less than a year, I had found twelve previously undocumented prairie and fen remnants. Some of them, though small, were of high quality.[5]

Ludlow's maps and notes showed that the biggest prairie in the region had been on what is now Wright-Patterson Air Force Base. I really wanted to look around there to see if there was anything left, but only those with valid security stickers on their vehicles could pass through the gate. I convinced my father, Gervais "Jerry" Nolin, to take me out there to look around. My father didn't know much about prairies, but he knew a lot about aviation and the base. Dad had been a P-51 pilot in the Pacific in World War II and was a champion model airplane builder for most of his adult life. He worked for many years at the Air Force Museum and later as a civilian contracting officer for the air force. Most importantly for the prairie research, he had the necessary sticker on his car. Perhaps he wondered where he went wrong in child-rearing as we drove through the offices, golf courses, residences, and flight line of the massive air force base looking for tall weeds.

It was September 1984 when we turned onto Pylon Road adjacent to the unmarked mown field where the Wright brothers had conducted their successful experiments. After a short distance, our efforts were rewarded by a tall clump of big bluestem prairie grass next to the ditch by the road. I was thrilled to find this bit of the past. Dad looked confused, pointed to a large field to our right, and inquired, "Well, what's all that?" There was an entire field of prairie grass waving in the breeze! It was a sight I never expected to see in Ohio. However, we both also noticed a yellow tractor with a mower on it methodically working its way across the prairie; within a few days it would likely have the entire field mowed down. When the machine approached our car, Dad and I waved to the operator, asking him to stop. When he turned off the tractor, we explained to him that this was a prairie and asked if he would refrain from mowing it for now. He was friendly enough but got on the radio and called his supervisor. After a while, the supervisor arrived and we gave him the same enthusiastic story. We must have been convincing, because the mower stayed off the rest of the day. Dad and I brainstormed about what we should do now. The next day he called the *Skywrighter*, the WPAFB newspaper, and explained, hoping to elicit a story, without success. I

Prairie remnant being mowed in September 1984.

checked around and found that Wright-Patterson had a natural resources manager, Terri Lucas. I gave her a call and told her about our discovery. Terri was genuinely interested, and shortly thereafter I walked the site with her. She worked with the base mowing crew to refrain from mowing until a decision was made on what to do with the prairie.

In spring 1985, naturalist and newspaper columnist Paul Knoop visited the newly discovered prairie remnant and wrote about it in his *Dayton Daily News* column:

> Walking out into the tall grasses is like walking back 200 years in time. One has a feeling of space and freedom because of the long vistas. The sky seemed "big" as they say in Montana, the "Big Sky Country." This feeling of expansiveness is perhaps the most special feature of this grassland community, a feeling that would be hard to duplicate elsewhere in southwest Ohio. As we walked forward pushing through the thick grass, we suddenly heard the bubbling, effervescent song of the male bobolink. We found ourselves surrounded by a colony of nesting bobolink and our binoculars were busy admiring the black and white patterned males. As one ornithologist stated, "The bobolink is the harlequin of the spring meadows. He is a happy-go-lucky fellow, with his suit of wrong-side up, the black below and the white above, a reckless, rollicking sort of a ways on a lark." We estimate the number of nesting pairs to be 40 to 50—an exceptional congregation for the Dayton area.[6]

Top: Presentation of Ohio Natural Landmark certificate to Wright-Patterson Air Force Base on February 24, 1986. Attendees are, from left, David Nolin; Dane Mutter of the Park District of Dayton-Montgomery County; Jan Williams and Dick Moseley of the Ohio Department of Natural Resources (ODNR); Colonel Charles E. Fox, commander of Wright-Patterson Air Force Base (WPAFB); Paul Knoop, education supervisor at Aullwood Audubon Center and Farm (AACF); Joseph Sommers, director of ODNR; Charity Krueger, director of AACF; Terri Lucas, natural resources manager, WPAFB.

Bottom: Sign installed by WPAFB in 1986 for the newly designated Huffman Prairie State Natural Landmark.

Later that year, Terri contacted the Ohio Department of Natural Resources Division of Natural Areas and Preserves to ask them for some advice about what we were calling Huffman Prairie. Assistant Chief Guy L. Denny suggested that Wright-Patterson apply to have the prairie designated a state natural landmark.[7] Terri filled out the paperwork and submitted it for consideration. After some discussion, base officials went ahead with the proposal. An award ceremony was arranged, and on February 24, 1986, Joe Sommers, the director of the Ohio Department of Natural Resources, presented the designation plaque to base commander Colonel Charles E. Fox.[8] The Ohio Natural Landmark designation was, and is, strictly voluntary and does not restrict in any way what the base does with the prairie. It does however, show Wright-Patterson's commitment to protecting the site. Later that year, WPAFB surveyors identified a 109-acre tract that would be designated on the base's plans and maps as the Huffman Prairie State Natural Landmark (HPSNL).

An excellent question is how did a large prairie remnant survive on a piece of land that underwent extensive impacts from over eighty years of draining, grazing, and tilling and over seventy years as part of a major air force base? Most prairie remnants survived because they were too wet, too dry, too rocky, too steep, or too hard to access to make good farmland.[9] The best prairie remnants in Ohio are on sites that made poor farmland. The oak openings in northwest Ohio are on a sand substrate that used to be part of a larger Lake Erie. The hillside prairies in Adams County are on hilly land with bedrock near the surface. However, the mesic prairies of western Ohio were relatively flat; contained rich, black soil; and were highly productive for agriculture once plowed. Thus by the time the Prairie Survey Project was started in 1974, there were few remaining examples of them in the state.

Most mesic prairie remnants in Ohio are either cemetery prairies or railroad corridor prairies. Cemetery prairies, such as the Smith and Bigelow pioneer cemeteries in Madison County, were unintentionally protected by pioneers soon after they arrived in the wilderness. The only pieces of prairie sod not subsequently plowed up were the tiny patches where the pioneers buried their dead. If they are not subsequently sprayed or overly mowed, these tiny plots can harbor impressive remnants of the once vast mesic prairies.[10] Railroad corridor prairie remnants are another accidental conservation mechanism. When the early railroads were laid out starting in the 1850s, they included rights-of-way, strips of land on either side managed by the railroad, not by the adjacent private landowners. If the railroad was laid out originally in a natural prairie, the right-of-way protected a thin strip of original prairie parallel to the tracks. If these are not overly sprayed, they can harbor great biodiversity. Excellent examples of railroad corridor prairies in Ohio are the Milford Center Prairie State Natural Area in Madison County and the Claridon Prairie in Marion County.[11]

In 1986, the remnant prairie vegetation of the new state natural landmark consisted of a series of large and small patches of prairie vegetation, mostly in the northern half of the site. The prairie patches were thick with native grasses including Indian grass, big bluestem, little bluestem, and prairie cordgrass. Twenty-four types of flowering plant species characteristic of Ohio prairies had been identified. However, many species characteristic of high-quality Ohio prairie remnants

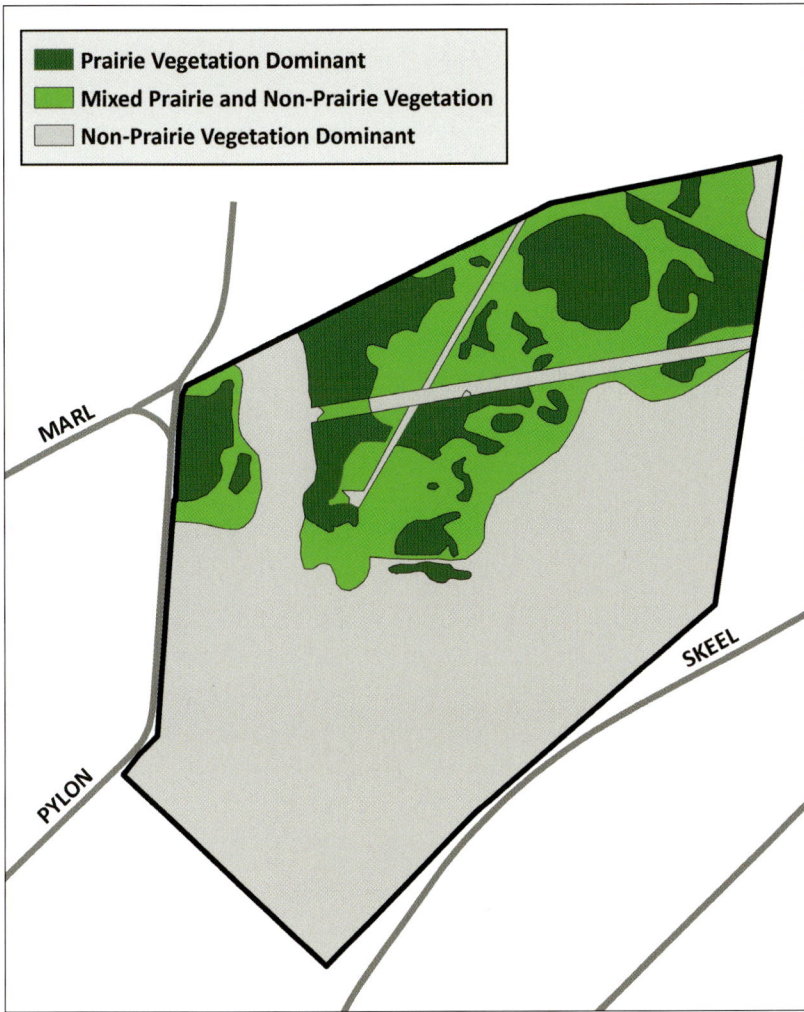

Prairie vegetation observed on HPSNL in 1986.

Legend:
- **Prairie Vegetation Dominant**
- **Mixed Prairie and Non-Prairie Vegetation**
- **Non-Prairie Vegetation Dominant**

were missing, and the prairie patches were surrounded by a matrix of nonnative pasture and hay grasses.

This remnant was not a cemetery or centered on a railroad right-of-way. The details of how it survived may never be known, but it seems likely that it was a big piece of the original prairie that had been traditionally used to pasture livestock and cut hay since the early 1800s. Using native prairies for haying and pasture was a common practice throughout the Midwest after Europeans settled the land. John E. Weaver conducted extensive research into the effects of grazing and clipping on these native pastures and in 1968 described them in detail in his now classic publication on prairie ecology, *Prairie Plants and Their Environment*.[12] Weaver described how native prairie communities responded to varying degrees of clipping and grazing by livestock. This grazing occurred where the animals were confined to fenced pastures; lightly pastured or clipped prairies could retain most of their biodiversity, while heavily grazed native pastures could lose most of it over time. Weaver described how species increase or decrease under varying amounts of grazing. In 1986, the flora of the new Huffman Prairie State Natural Landmark exhibited the qualities of an overgrazed prairie pasture:

- Decreased diversity and cover of palatable native species.
- Increased diversity and cover of unpalatable native and nonnative species such as ironweed (*Vernonia gigantea*), yarrow (*Achillea millefolium*), and wild parsnip (*Pastinaca sativa*).
- Increased cover of nonnative cool season hay and pasture grasses such as Kentucky bluegrass (*Poa pratensis*), timothy (*Phleum pretense*), and smooth brome (*Bromus inermis*).

In addition to damage by past grazing, overcutting, and regular mowing, the new state natural landmark also contained several narrow corridors of disturbed soil and weedy vegetation that marked the beds of the abandoned Dayton-Springfield Pike and the former Yellow Springs–Clifton Pike. A wide corridor of disturbed soil marked the path of the large buried concrete tiles that had been installed in 1942 to drain the groundwater from the runways. Another line of disturbed soil marks the course of the former speed course, and another the course of a large drainage ditch that the army filled in after 1915.[13]

Prescribed burn on HPSNL in March 1988, by WPAFB Fire Department.

Initially it was hoped that the return of fire would solve these problems. Fire kills or damages woody trees and shrubs, invigorates prairie vegetation, and induces many prairie species to germinate or produce more seed. In 1988, Terri Lucas worked with the WPAFB Fire Department to burn a piece of the prairie, perhaps the first time the prairie had been burned in nearly two hundred years. The results were impressive the first year after this burn, with lush growth by the prairie vegetation where it already dominated. However, the fire did not seem to have much impact on the degraded sections, which continued to have little evident native prairie vegetation.

At this point, the project changed from a protection or preservation effort into a restoration effort. I guess I have to take the blame or credit for that: my recent research of local prairie and fen remnants had enlightened me to the diversity and beauty of these pieces of the past. Huffman Prairie seemed to offer a great opportunity to restore a large prairie, not just a tiny fragment. The prairie was large, grew from its original black soil, and had impressive nesting bird, insect, and native plant populations. Why not bring back some of the missing pieces?

The local prairies seemed to have had a character and composition somewhat different from those in other parts of Ohio, so it made sense to only use local plants or seeds in the restoration effort. However, there was no place to purchase local seeds in the necessary quantities. Collecting and redistributing seed from local prairie remnants and Huffman Prairie itself seemed logical, but that was easier said than done. While an enjoyable fall activity, handpicking the seeds of prairie plants was not a very productive way to get enough seed for a large restoration.

Fortunately, the art and science of restoring and planting tallgrass prairies was starting to bloom farther to the west. A fledgling company

Steve Apfelbaum of Applied Ecological Services explaining prairie seed cleaning and storage to Alex Shartle of the Park District of Dayton-Montgomery County in 1988. Photo taken in Brodhead, Wisconsin.

in southern Wisconsin called Applied Ecological Services (AES), headed by an enthusiastic young man named Steve Apfelbaum, was doing innovative prairie restoration work. Steve graciously agreed to host a group from the Park District of Dayton–Montgomery County, give us a tour of their facilities, and give us some advice on harvesting the seeds of prairie plants. In the fall of 1988, I took a trip to AES with Alex Shartle, the park manager for the district, who had originally infected me with prairie fever. We loaded a truck with camping supplies and set off for Wisconsin. When we arrived, we found an enthusiastic group of young people who had acquired an old farm and converted it into a center for prairie restoration. The old barn had many bags of seed hanging from the rafters to keep them away from mice, several pieces of farm equipment were being converted to harvest and clean prairie seed, and nearby were some pretty impressive stands of planted mesic prairie. They had modified an old Allis-Chalmers farm combine to harvest prairie grasses. Most modern combines are not capable of harvesting prairie grasses, because these seeds are too light and fluffy. AES had discovered that this older model gleaner combine could do an exceptional job if adjusted properly. They showed us how to adjust and operate their gleaner until we got the hang of it somewhat, and they gave plenty of great advice on how to properly dry, store, and plant the seeds. We were both anxious to take home what we had learned from Steve, whom Alex described as a "genius in a T-shirt."

The next fall I found a local farm implement dealer who had one of these old combines, and he volunteered to help us try it on Huffman Prairie. It worked great, harvesting about 750 pounds of prairie grass seed. In 1990, the Park District purchased its own combine. There was not enough money budgeted to buy the machine, so Alex pulled some strings and raided the budget of one of the parks, and the manager of that park found that he no longer had the money to put the sides on a new horse barn. That did not go over well, but we had the combine! Our goals were to continue harvesting seed from Huffman Prairie to use for restoration of its degraded sections and to create fields of prairie grass on several park district reserves.

Our new-old combine was a very tricky and temperamental machine that needed a practiced hand to operate and maintain. Fortunately, the park district had the right person for the job, the Carriage Hill Farm park manager, Pete Smith. Pete was an experienced farmer and mechanic who volunteered to help with the prairie harvest project. He was also a joker, constantly trying to play tricks on everyone, usually at the expense of their dignity. He had a gift for saying outrageous or off-color things no one else could get away with.

The time to harvest prairie grass seed in southwest Ohio is early October. The prairie grasses take on rich fall colors, and the dried seed lingers for a short time on the end of the long stalks. There is a narrow harvest window, so we were anxious to get the combine to the prairie and get started. This commute turned out to be an adventure. Our gleaner was at the district's Germantown Reserve, on the other side of Dayton to the southwest. There was no trailer or truck to haul it, so Pete resolved to drive it to Huffman Prairie. He took it up back roads while we followed him in a pickup. Being a practical man, Pete took the shortest route, which happened to go northeastward right through the mansion district of Oakwood, an affluent suburb south of Dayton. It was a weird sight, the noisy old monster puffing down the street past giant homes, barely missing the expensive cars parked near the street. As we neared the air force base and Pete turned onto Springfield Street, Kevin Kepler, the other park district employee in the truck with me, said, "Oh my God, there's no way that thing will fit through the narrow bridge up there!" We passed Pete and zoomed to the bridge underpass. We looked at it and then at the rapidly approaching combine. Kevin was right, no way! A wreck was about to happen. We got on the radio and called Pete and stood there waving our hands. Pete just grinned and, if anything, accelerated. The old machine flew through the underpass with no more than two inches on either side and didn't get or make a scratch. Pete laughed loudly, taking great amusement in our panic. The combine finally arrived safely at the prairie on Wright-Patterson, but Kevin and I had our first gray hairs.

It was time to adjust the machine to harvest prairie grass, and Pete knew just what to do. He crawled underneath, hammering and cursing, adjusting screens, and carefully lubricating all the joints. When we started it and drove through the wine- and copper-colored fall grasses, it immediately began to collect large quantities of seed. By the end of the next day, we had filled most of the bin. However, when we tried to use the combine's auger to transfer the seed to a Park District truck, nothing happened. The auger was built to move dense grain, not fluffy prairie grass seed. Pete handed Kevin a shovel handle and instructed him to climb into the combine's seed bin and use the stick to force the seed into the auger. The sight of Kevin straddling the bin and jamming the seed into the whirling auger below him would have raised a lot of red flags with the Occupational Safety and Health Administration. Fortunately, it worked out, and Kevin kept all of his limbs. He had augered about 950 pounds of seed into the back of a Park District dump truck.

The seed was moist and smelled sweetly of cut hay. It was spread out to dry on the floor of a Park District barn. When dry, the seed was bagged and stored for planting the following spring. We now had the means to

Mary Klunk operating the Park District's new-old combine in 1992. The combine has since been replaced by smaller seed harvesters that are pulled behind a tractor; each of these units contains a rotating brush with short spines that whisk the seeds into a bin.

Pete Smith, David Nolin, and Kevin Kepler of the Park District of Dayton-Montgomery County auger prairie grass seed, harvested from the combine, into a truck, 1991.

Pete Smith of the Park District of Dayton-Montgomery County (left) and volunteers for The Nature Conservancy spreading the freshly harvested seeds of big bluestem and Indian grass to dry on the floor of the replica 1905 Wright Brothers hangar, 1991.

obtain abundant prairie grass seed to help restore the degraded sections of the prairie and to plant parkland into native grasses.

However, restoring the prairie posed some scientific, practical, and ethical questions:

- Is there a seed bank—seeds of any of the missing prairie plants present in the soil of the degraded sections that could potentially germinate and restore themselves without reseeding?
- If not, how can native vegetation be restored without damaging the excellent nesting bird and insect populations?
- We now had access to bulk quantities of native grass seeds, but a prairie contains scores of flowering plant species (forbs) that should be a part of a restoration. Where would this seed come from?
- Where will the labor and funds to restore the prairie come from?

Fortunately, the restoration effort got a big boost in 1990 with the help of The Nature Conservancy (TNC), the national private conservation group. In December 1988, that organization entered into a cooperative agreement with the U.S. Department of Defense to inventory and manage unique natural areas on military bases.[14] In 1990, TNC's Ohio chapter participated in this national effort by entering into a cooperative agreement with Wright-Patterson Air Force Base to design and implement a management plan for Huffman Prairie. A corps of volunteers was organized to do the necessary labor, with TNC staff providing technical assistance and a volunteer coordinator, with some financial assistance supplied by WPAFB. The restoration effort became a partnership between TNC, the park district, and WPAFB. Between 1990 and 2002, TNC and its volunteers did important work that greatly benefitted the prairie and its restoration.

TNC's first major undertaking was to conduct inventories of the prairie's plant and animal life. They correctly made the point that you can't manage something properly if you don't have a good handle on what is there. To allow for proper monitoring and management, TNC installed a grid of metal reference posts in the prairie and divided it into four management quadrants. TNC staff, volunteers, and private and academic researchers all contributed to the inventory effort.

This research provided good news and bad news about the health of the prairie:

- A study of nesting birds from 1990 to 1998 revealed healthy populations of seven declining bird species that are dependent on the availability of large grasslands like Huffman Prairie: bobolink, dickcissel, Henslow's sparrow, grasshopper sparrow, savannah sparrow, eastern meadowlark, and sedge wren.[15]
- An inventory of lepidoptera (butterflies and moths) found 22 species of butterflies and 231 of moths.[16] Subsequent moth research identified 28 moth species never before documented in Ohio, 3 of which were new to science.[17]
- The baseline plant survey identified 178 species of plants on the prairie. Of these, 115 were native and 63 were introduced from other parts of the country or the world. The native species included 47 species now known to be important components of an Ohio prairie.[18]
- A study to determine whether a seed bank was present in the soil of the degraded sections was not encouraging; results showed no significant presence of plant species that were not already present in the vegetation.[19]
- Analysis of random plots found that while native vegetation was thick in patches, much of the site was dominated by nonnative plants.

This research led to the first management plan for Huffman Prairie in 1994. It had three main goals:

1. To restore the plant diversity in the prairie and bring it back to a condition similar to what existed in the 1800s (based on best available

Left: WPAFB staff plowing a nine-acre portion of HPSNL that was not expressing native vegetation, 1993. TNC volunteers subsequently hand-broadcasted locally collected seeds onto the black prairie soil.

Below: After five years, the section that was plowed and planted had become a beautiful display of prairie vegetation native to the local area.

records from Van Cleve and other botanists from that era and the flora of other nearby prairie remnants).

2. To maintain the diversity of nesting grassland birds and prairie lepidoptera (butterflies and moths).
3. To use it as a setting for educating the general public about the natural history of Huffman Prairie.[20]

The restoration plan was a collaboration, but Nature Conservancy volunteers did much of the fieldwork, harvesting, cleaning, storing, and planting seed; cutting and pulling invasive species; and planting plugs of prairie plants into degraded sections.

In 1992 and 1993, the restoration partnership resolved to till and reseed a nine-acre section of the Huffman Prairie State Natural Landmark that was not expressing prairie vegetation, even after having been burned in early spring. Wright-Patterson staff plowed the black soil, and TNC volunteers hand-spread a diverse mix of locally collected forb, or flower, seeds mixed with grass seeds harvested with the combine. The seed was then lightly worked into the soil. Within five years, these plantings grew into an impressive display of prairie vegetation native to the Dayton area.

A gentler approach was taken in sections of HPSNL that contained significant amounts of remnant prairie vegetation. In addition to controlling unwanted vegetation, diversity was enhanced by reestablishing "missing" prairie species that could be found on other nearby prairie remnants. Seeds were collected from these areas in the fall. Some seeds were planted directly into restoration areas, and others were grown into seedlings at the Park District's Ohio Prairie Seed Nursery at Germantown Reserve, which TNC volunteers later planted in the prairie. Seedlings were also planted in a "prairie garden" near the 1905 hangar replica for an educational display.

TNC tried several different methods to restore degraded sections of the prairie. In general, planting and reseeding efforts where the compe-

TNC volunteers transplanting greenhouse-grown seedlings of prairie plants at the Park District's Ohio Prairie Seed Nursery greenhouse at Germantown Reserve (now Germantown MetroPark), 1994.

Volunteers for the Ohio Chapter of The Nature Conservancy planting plugs of native prairie forbs at HPSNL, 1994.

TNC volunteer digging out autumn olive shrub on HPSNL, 1995.

tition had been reduced or eliminated had good results. Planting directly in sites that contained significant amounts of cool-season grasses like smooth brome and tough weeds like wild parsnip and poison hemlock had poor success. Some progress was made by cutting or pulling invasive weeds and shrubs, but in many cases, they soon returned. To help with these projects, TNC organized a large volunteer workday each spring as part of a statewide effort, "Restore Ohio."

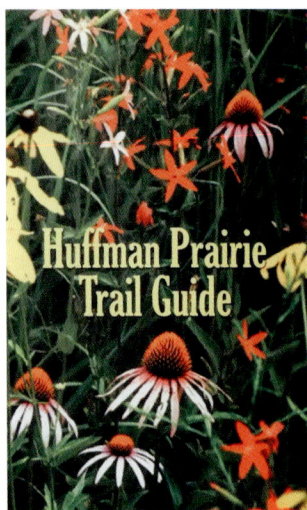

Above: Cover of first interpretive trail guide for HPSNL.

Right: Base commander Colonel William B. Orellana presents Ron and Liz Cramer, Terry Seidel, and Irv Bieser of The Nature Conservancy with a certificate of achievement in 1995.

One of the biggest successes of these volunteer efforts was the increased awareness and appreciation of the site. TNC laid out and installed a new interpretive trail through the prairie in 1994, making the interior of the site accessible to visitors for the first time. The partnership also produced a colorful new brochure to help with the interpretation. Other notable successes were the excellent baseline research completed, and the development of a management plan approved by the managing partners.

In 1995, TNC volunteer leaders Ron and Liz Cramer received a certificate of achievement from Wright-Patterson Air Force Base for their leadership in the prairie restoration effort.[21] In 1996, they received The Nature Conservancy's National President's Stewardship Award for their "exemplary volunteer leadership, and patient labor."[22]

In 2002, TNC discontinued its participation in the restoration efforts at Huffman Prairie. Unfortunately, this resulted in a decrease in management activity for several years, which raised concerns that any ground gained was being lost. In 2007, WPAFB engaged the firm Amec Earth and Environmental, Inc. to evaluate the prairie again and produce a revised management plan. This study found that much of the designated prairie was still dominated by nonnative plants. Amec divided the prairie into three categories: "Healthy Areas" of prairie vegetation covered 7 percent of the site, "Intermediate Areas" covered about 23 percent, and "Degraded Areas" covered 70 percent.[23] Amec recommended a more aggressive approach to the restoration. By far the biggest obstacle to restoration of the site was the abundance of smooth brome grass, a European hay/pasture grass. This aggressive species produces a thick sod that prevents other

WPAFB crew spraying patches of nonnative vegetation at HPSNL.

Green prairie grasses coming up through dead patches of smooth brome following herbicide application.

Vigorous growth of native prairie grasses following a spring burn and herbicide application.

Mary Klunk of Five Rivers MetroParks loading the seed drill with locally collected seeds of prairie plants, 2014.

No-till seed drill planting prairie seeds into a patch of HPSNL that had been treated with herbicide in early spring, 2014.

species from becoming established.[24] Other invasive "weeds" that prevented restoration included wild parsnip and poison hemlock. Unless these species were controlled, large-scale progress was unlikely.

In 2008, Five Rivers MetroParks (formerly the Park District of Dayton-Montgomery County) and WPAFB resolved to initiate an aggressive restoration effort on the southeast quarter of HPSNL. That March, the WPAFB Fire Department burned the entire section. In early April, WPAFB personnel sprayed the section with the herbicide glyphosate to kill the brome and other nonnative plants that come up early in the spring, before most native species have made significant growth. That summer it became clear that an early spring glyphosate application had a significant beneficial effect. Released from the brome turf, native grasses and some forbs grew thickly from suppressed native plants that were already there or from the seed bank. Over the next three years, the other three sections of the prairie were similarly treated with glyphosate in early spring, with similar results.

It seemed we had identified a process to help the prairie restore itself. The use of glyphosate was carefully considered and would not be a recommendation for all prairie restorations. Glyphosate is not selective and can kill any green vegetation it is applied to. However, if the timing, rate, and location of the application is right, it can be an important tool in restoring a degraded prairie.

Amec had also identified an eight-acre corner of the prairie that was especially devoid of native plant species. This section was also sprayed with glyphosate in the early spring of 2008, but here Five Rivers Metro-Parks planted a diverse mix of seed collected from local prairie remnants, using its no-till seed drill. This planting appeared a failure at first, but after five years and a burn, it became an excellent prairie restoration that included seed bank species as well as those that had been planted.

In 2011, about eight acres of the northeast corner of the original Huffman Prairie State Natural Landmark were lost to provide space for an explosive disposal range the air force needed for Patterson Field. To mitigate this loss, WPAFB expanded HPSNL on the south end by eleven

A restored section of Huffman Prairie State Natural Landmark in midsummer.

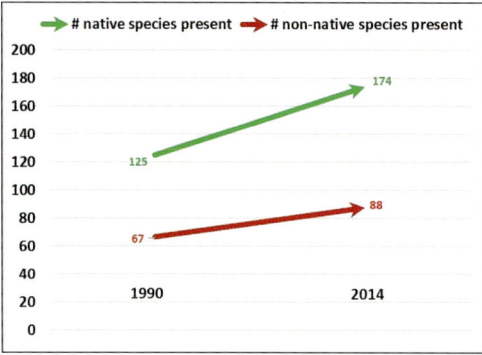

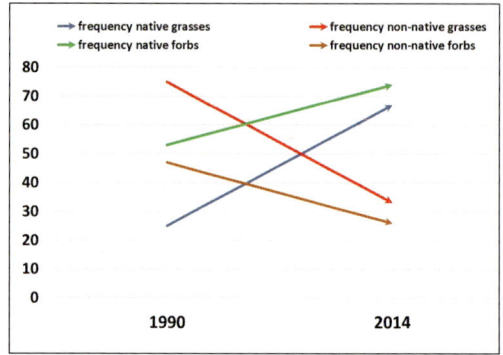

Above left:
Changes in plant
composition on
HPSNL between
1990 and 2014.

Above right:
Frequency of
native and nonna-
tive grasses and
forbs on HPSNL in
1990 and 2014.

Right: Restora-
tion progress
on HPSNL as of
2016.

acres. The portion that was lost contained some of the best parts of the
original prairie remnant, while the new portion contained only scattered
prairie vegetation. In the spring of 2014, Five Rivers MetroParks over-
seeded a diverse mix of locally collected prairie seeds into this section
with the agency's seed drill.

To evaluate the effectiveness of the various restoration efforts, in 2014
Five Rivers MetroParks engaged biologist David Minney to conduct a
plant community monitoring study and a breeding bird census of Huffman Prairie State Natural Landmark. Minney had completed these same
studies on the prairie in 1990 while working for The Nature Conservancy.
In his 2014 report, he documented the native and nonnative grasses and
forbs species present and compared these numbers to the 1990 results.
He also documented the frequency that different species were encountered

and compared these results to 1990's. His report confirmed the progress made to date in restoring the diversity and composition of HPSNL to a mesic prairie plant community, with greatly increased frequency and cover of native species and greatly decreased frequency and cover of nonnative species. He also found that new challenges to the restoration effort had appeared, including an increase in woody vegetation and a large increase of a native forb, Canada goldenrod (*Solidago altissima*).[25]

One of the most surprising results of the recent management efforts has been the appearance of new species from the seed bank, even though previous research had indicated there probably was no seed bank. Rare or unusual prairie species that have appeared on their own since the

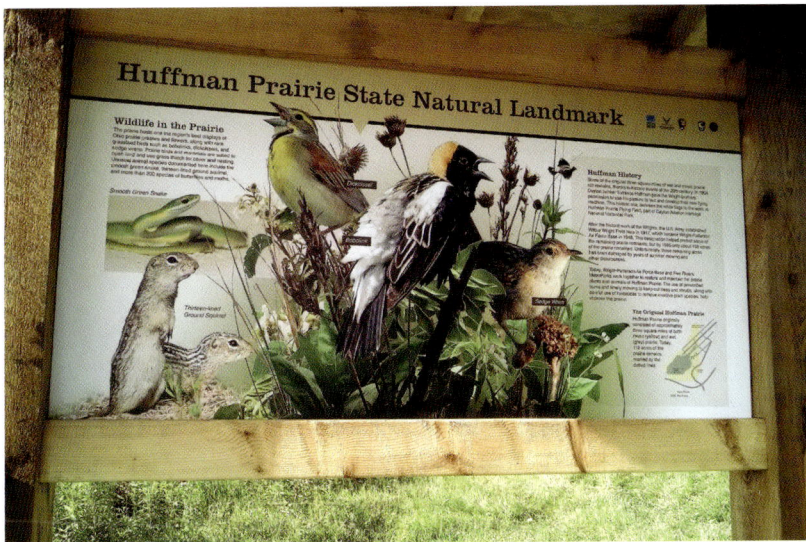

Interpretive kiosk installed on HPSNL in 2015.

Controlled burn on HPSNL by WPAFB staff and Fire Department, and U.S. Fish and Wildlife Service in November 2016.

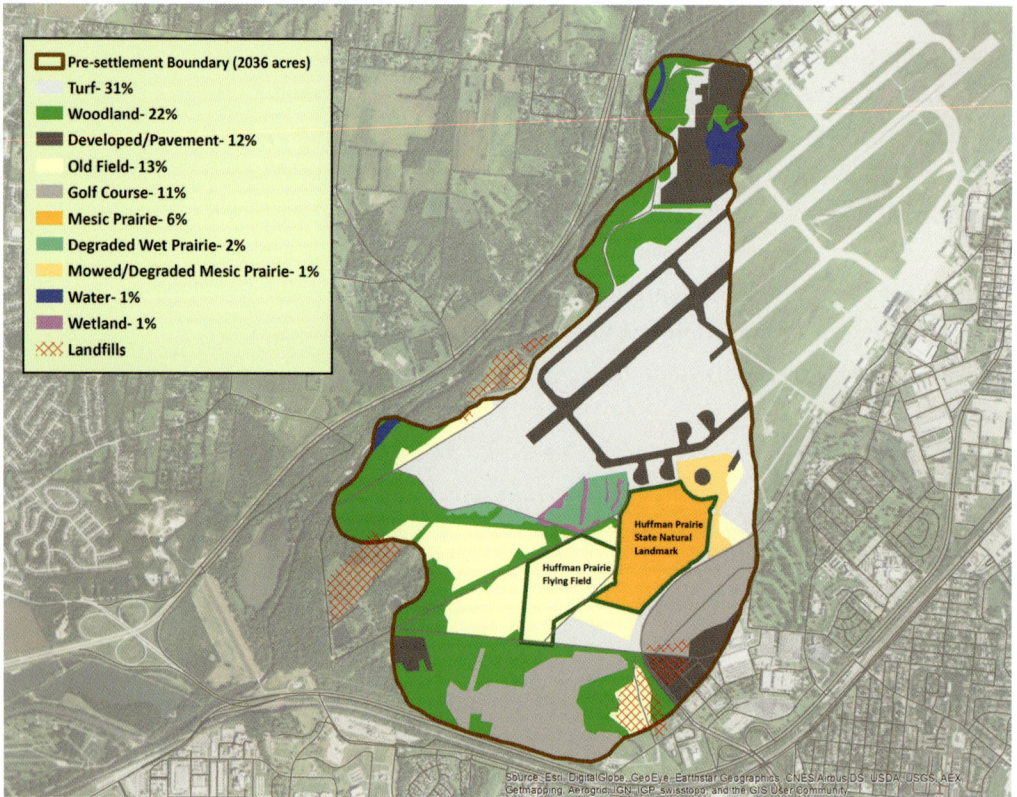

Legend:
- Pre-settlement Boundary (2036 acres)
- Turf- 31%
- Woodland- 22%
- Developed/Pavement- 12%
- Old Field- 13%
- Golf Course- 11%
- Mesic Prairie- 6%
- Degraded Wet Prairie- 2%
- Mowed/Degraded Mesic Prairie- 1%
- Water- 1%
- Wetland- 1%
- Landfills

Huffman Prairie State Natural Landmark

Huffman Prairie Flying Field

Source: Esri, DigitalGlobe, GeoEye, Earthstar Geographics, CNES/Airbus DS, USDA, USGS, AEX, Getmapping, Aerogrid, IGN, IGP, swisstopo, and the GIS User Community

Land use on presettlement Huffman Prairie in 2016.

glyphosate applications include scurf pea (*Orbexilum onobrychis*), pale-spike lobelia (*Lobelia spicata*), slender foxglove (*Agalinis tenuifolia*), smooth aster (*Symphyotrichum laeve*), nodding lady's tresses orchid (*Spiranthes ovalis*), and western tansy mustard (*Descurainia pinnata*). The rarest species found to date, first observed in 2016, was a population of the state-endangered northern adder's-tongue fern (*Ophioglossum pusillum*).

Since 2015, Huffman Prairie State Natural Landmark has been managed by a partnership that includes Wright-Patterson Air Force Base, Five Rivers MetroParks, and the U.S. Fish and Wildlife Service. The actions these partners undertake must be in compliance with the Integrated Natural Resources Management Plan for Wright-Patterson Air Force Base. This plan takes into account federal and state laws and the numerous priorities that exist on a major air force base.[26]

One possibility that has been discussed by the managing partners is the restoration of a portion of the wet prairie and fen habitat that once covered much of WPAFB west of HPSNL. Most of this habitat has been lost to runway construction, drainage, and past agricultural use, but the thick peat soils are still there. The groundwater continues to flow through culverts, tiles, and ditches. Where regular mowing has been discontinued and field tile has broken down, a few small sections have come back. This suggests that larger-scale restoration is possible. If the plan designed to be compatible with the active airfield and other activities on WPAFB, a significant piece of the former wet prairie and fen could be restored, given the time and necessary resources. Fortunately, there are two nearby outstanding remnants of this rare plant community that could supply a model for a restoration. Siebenthaler Fen in the Beaver Creek State Wildlife Area, six miles to the southeast, and Leadingham Prairie Preserve, managed by the Clark County Park District, six miles to the north, are both excellent examples of fens occurring in flat, buried river valleys.[27]

Until 2015, the interpretation of the Huffman Prairie State Natural Landmark had been limited. In 2014, a ranger with the National Park Service, Leisa Ling, had proposed that NPS and Five Rivers MetroParks submit a grant application to the Ohio Environmental Education Fund to obtain funding to improve HPSNL interpretation. The grant was awarded, covering the costs of developing and installing a kiosk and interpretive signage and producing a new brochure.[28] The new signs were installed and dedicated in September of that year.

The prairies of southwestern Ohio were complex habitats that are at best only partially understood. Huffman Prairie State Natural Landmark, a site damaged by human activities and invaded by plant species from many parts of the world, has been and continues to be a restoration challenge. It is probably not possible to fully restore it to its 1795 condition, as it was when Benjamin Van Cleve first visited Huffman Prairie. Annual uncontrolled fires no longer sweep over the landscape, there are no herds of grazing bison, the drainage has been altered, and many plant species from other parts of the country and world are now present. Even so, the prairie's diversity and beauty are inspiring, and the bobolinks and smooth green snakes don't seem to mind if there are some nonnative plants in the mix. The prairie continues to harbor a diversity of life that has been on-site for thousands of years, a richness still being discovered. It also contains some carefully reestablished species that had been lost to human impact. Here, people are slowly discovering how to renew and manage a lost piece of our shared natural heritage, albeit a new version that can function in a world changed by human beings. I like to think that Wilbur and Orville would approve.

CHAPTER SEVEN

Plants and Animals of Huffman Prairie State Natural Landmark

The south end of Patterson Field on Wright-Patterson Air Force Base is home to a diversity of bird species. As of June 9, 2017, birders have reported observing 179 species of birds in the vicinity of the Huffman Prairie Flying Field and the Huffman Prairie State Natural Landmark (HPSNL).[1]

Some of the rarest birds found in the state are grassland species, declining in Ohio because large grasslands are becoming increasingly uncommon. The best place to see these species in the Dayton area is HPSNL, a fine example of an Ohio grassland. For this reason, land management plans for the site have always been designed to provide habitat for grassland species. However, a staggered mowing and burning plan can leave some small trees and brambles in at least one quarter of the site each year, which can accommodate many other species.

The avian star of the grassland nesting bird community at HPSNL is the bobolink. These black, white, and yellow performers are actually a type of blackbird. Bobolinks nest in the northern United States and southern Canada but spend the winter on the grasslands of southern South America.[2] Bobolinks arrive at Huffman Prairie in early May and immediately stake out their sections. The promiscuous males sing mostly when in flight, a melodic yet sort of mechanical jumble of sounds. By the end of July, the adults and young fledglings gather into small flocks that roam about the prairie until late September, when they head south. Bobolinks need large grasslands without significant woody vegetation.

Two distinctive grassland birds with black, yellow, and brown coloration that nest on the prairie are the Eastern meadowlark and the dickcissel. Meadowlarks, also a type of blackbird, are regular nesters on the prairie.

Clockwise from top left: Male bobolink (*Dolichonyx oryzivorus*) at HPSNL. Female bobolink at HPSNL. Eastern meadowlark (*Sturnella magna*) at HPSNL. Dickcissel (*Spiza americana*) at HPSNL.

They have a distinctive two-part whistling song and a chattering call. Dickcissels, relatives of the familiar northern cardinal, are common nesters on the prairie in some years, but in other years there are none. The male has a short, staccato call that sounds somewhat like this bird's name.

At least six types of sparrow call the prairie home during the year. Three grassland species regularly breed on the prairie: the grasshopper, savannah, and Henslow's sparrow. Each of these has declined significantly in Ohio in recent years, due to loss of grassland habitat.[3] Grasshopper and savannah sparrows prefer sections with shorter grass, but the Henslow's sparrow needs fields with matted grasses to nest in and scattered shrubs to sing from. The song sparrow and the chipping sparrow are less particular about where they live and are common in a variety of grassy and brushy habitats. American tree sparrows (*Spizella arborea*) arrive in the fall and spend the winter in the area, including Huffman Prairie State Natural Landmark.

The sedge wren is a small and rare bird of prairies and sedge meadows. It has the unusual habit of arriving on the prairie in the middle of the summer to begin nesting, when the big bluestem is about one meter high. It especially prefers sites that were partially burned before the growing season; it builds its nest in the tall, robust stems rising from a burn, with dried grasses from the unburned sections.[4]

The upland sandpiper is a shorebird that prefers large grasslands with shorter grass. About the only place where these conditions can be found in western Ohio are airports, where the birds perch on fences and posts and give their gurgling whistle of a song. They spend the winter on the grasslands of southern South America, migrating to the midwestern United States in May. Upland sandpipers regularly nest on Patterson Field and may have done so on HPSNL in 2017.

Clockwise from top left: Grasshopper sparrow (*Ammodramus savannarum*) at HPSNL. Henslow's sparrow (*Ammodramus henslowii*). Photo by Marge Bicknell. Savannah sparrow (*Passerculus sandwichensis*). Photo by Marge Bicknell. Song sparrow (*Melospiza melodia*) at HPSNL.

Clockwise from top left: Field sparrow (*Spizella pusilla*) at HPSNL. Chipping sparrow (*Spizella passerina*) at HPSNL. Upland sandpiper (*Bartramia longicauda*) perched on the security fence on the boundary of the HPSNL. Photo by Rick Luehrs. Sedge wren (*Cistothorus platensis*) at HPSNL. Photo by Jim McCormac.

In mid-July, ruby-throated hummingbirds venture from nearby woodlands and descend on the prairie in good numbers to drink nectar from the blossoms of royal catchfly. This spectacular scarlet-flowered plant is often pollinated by hummers. The action is fast, as dozens of hummingbirds zoom from plant to plant, but they are not tolerant of other hummingbirds and spend a good portion of their time chasing the competition.

The blue grosbeak is a beautiful blue bird with a very large beak and chestnut wing bars that has been spreading into southwestern Ohio from the south. It now nests on the prairie, particularly where roses and brambles give some cover. Another blue bird that likes a brushy prairie is the indigo bunting, which is smaller than the grosbeak and has a metallic sheen to its blue feathers. It is easy to see these birds or hear their loud series of two-syllable notes in the spring and summer near the trail kiosk. Willow flycatchers and American goldfinches also favor brushy grasslands and borders.

Two of the most common nesting birds are the common yellowthroat and the red-winged blackbird. The common yellowthroat is a type of warbler that also likes brushy sections of the prairie, where the males sing a loud *wichety-wichety-wichety* in spring and summer. The male has a bright yellow throat and a black face mask. The female is olive brown with some brighter yellow feathers on the throat and under the tail. Male red-winged blackbirds are unmistakable, with black plumage offset by red and yellow shoulder badges, and a loud *conk-la-reee!*

Swallows are common all summer over Huffman Prairie State Natural Landmark. Barn swallows nest in the replica of the 1905 hangar, and mix with tree swallows, cliff swallows (*Petrochelidon pyrrhonota*),

Clockwise from top left: Ruby-throated hummingbird (*Archilochus colubris*) at HPSNL. Photo by Jim McCormac. Blue grosbeak (*Passerina caerulea*) at HPSNL. Indigo bunting (*Passerina cyanea*). Photo by Dan Enders. Willow flycatcher (*Empidonax traillii*) at HPSNL. American goldfinches (*Spinus tristis*) at HPSNL.

and rough-winged swallows (*Stelgidopteryx serripennis*) as they hunt for the abundant small insects above the grassland on summer evenings.

Most of the grassland birds that nest on HPSNL head south for the winter, but some species arrive for the winter from the north or stay for a while when migrating south in the fall and north in the spring. These include three beautiful birds of prey: the northern harrier, short-eared owl, and merlin. The first two species are of similar size and are only found in large open grasslands and wetlands where there are plenty of small mammals to eat. Northern harriers are regularly seen on the prairie between November and April. Sometimes called marsh hawks, these

Clockwise from top left: Red-winged blackbird (*Agelaius phoeniceus*) at HPSNL. Common yellowthroat *Geothlypis trichas*). Photo by Roger Garber. Eastern kingbird *Tyrannus tyrannus*) at HPSNL. Tree swallow (*Tachycineta bicolor*) at HPSNL. Barn swallow (*Hirundo rustica*) at HPSNL.

Above left: Northern harrier (*Circus cyaneus*) at HPSNL. Photo by Roger Garber.

Above right: Short-eared owl (*Asio flammeus*) at HPSNL. Photo by Chong Zhang.

Right: Merlin (*Falco columbarius*) at HPSNL. Photo by Rick Luehrs.

birds of prey used to nest on Huffman Prairie, as ornithologist Ben Blincoe documented: "This harrier, for many years, nested in the marshes at Wright-Patterson Air Force Base before these were drained in the 1930's. This locality in Greene County was visited by Mr. O. L. Cunningham and me May 6, 1928. We found three Marsh Hawk's nests, each containing three fresh eggs. Louis B. Kalter of Dayton banded several nestlings before drainage and aeronautical activities eliminated the habitat."[5]

Short-eared owls are irregular winter visitors and can be seen between November and March. Some years there may be none seen, but up to twenty of these distinctive owls spent much of the winter on Huffman Prairie State Natural Landmark in 2016. They perch on the ground and hunt near dawn and dusk for small mammals. Their flight pattern is distinctive, with deep, irregular beats. They constantly turn their heads in flight, to watch humans intruding on their hunting grounds.

Two other birds of prey, which can be seen any time of year on HPSNL, are the red-tailed hawk and the American kestrel. The red-tail is a large, soaring hawk that hunts for mammals such as meadow voles and cottontail rabbits. It usually builds its sturdy basketlike stick nest in a tall tree next to an open area. The kestrel is a small falcon that hunts grass-

Above left: Red-tailed hawk (*Buteo jamaicensis*) at HPSNL. Photo by Rick Luehrs.

Above right: American kestrel (*Falco sparverius*) at HPSNL. Photo by Rick Luehrs.

lands for meadow voles and other small mammals in the winter but takes a variety of large insects, such as grasshoppers, in the summer.

Patterson Field on Wright-Patterson Air Force Base is an important air base for the United States. Its large runway can accommodate very large aircraft and large numbers of modern aircraft. Since 2010, Patterson Field has been a major base for C-17 cargo aircraft.[6] An increasing problem for managers of military and civilian airports is bird-aircraft collisions, which can cause serious damage to or even result in the loss of aircraft. Traditionally, including at Patterson Field, land management around airports consists mainly of maintaining regularly mowed turfgrass. However, research has shown that this can actually increase bird species that pose some of the highest risk to aircraft, because turfgrass attracts large grazers such as Canada geese (*Branta canadensis*) that do not inhabit taller, unmown grasslands. Converting turfgrass around airports to prairie vegetation can result in fewer bird-aircraft collisions and can be an effective part of an airport management plan.[7]

Mammals that have been seen on Huffman Prairie State Natural Landmark in recent years include white-tailed deer, striped skunk (*Mephitis mephitis*), coyote (*Canis latrans*), red fox (*Vulpes vulpes*), groundhog, meadow vole, deer mouse, eastern mole (*Scalopus aquaticus*), eastern cottontail, and thirteen-lined ground squirrel.

The thirteen-lined ground squirrel, a true prairie animal, is often seen near the replica of the 1905 hangar. It spends most of its time in long burrows but will frequently look at the aboveground world by standing upright on the edge of a burrow. It can run extremely fast if caught away from the burrow and is good at changing directions while running. It has a trilled whistle call that, from a distance, sounds like a tiny bell ringing.

A very rare mammal that has been documented on the prairie has an interesting story. The Indiana bat, or Indiana Myotis, is listed as an endangered species by the federal government. The entire population of these small, dark-colored bats spends the winter in a small number of moist caves scattered throughout the species' range.[8] Here the bats hibernate in large, closely packed clusters that can contain thousands of individuals. In spring, these congregations break up and the bats disperse to breed in woodlands that have suitable trees. Maternal

Clockwise from top left: Deer mouse (*Peromyscus maniculatus*) at HPSNL. Meadow vole (*Microtus pennsylvanicus*). Photo by Jim McCormac. Eastern cottontail (*Sylvilagus floridanus*) at HPSNL. Fox squirrel (*Sciurus niger*) at HPSNL. Photo by Rick Luehrs. Groundhog (*Marmota monax*) at HPSNL. Photo by Roger Garber.

White-tailed deer (*Odocoileus virginianus*) at HPSNL. Photo by Roger Garber.

Right: Thirteen-lined ground squirrel (*Spermophilus tridecemlineatus*) at HPSNL. Photo by Roger Garber.

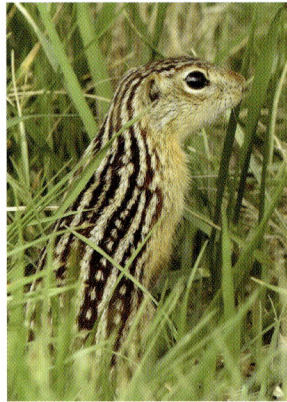

Far right: Indiana bat (*Myotis sodalis*).

groupings of females will bear young together in one or more large trees that contain peeling bark, which they shelter under. Because the Indiana bat is a federally endangered species, Wright-Patterson Air Force Base monitors the population on the base. In 2000, researchers working for WPAFB netted two Indiana bats on the base over Trout Creek, next to HPSNL. These individuals were fitted with tiny radio transmitters and released. These researchers soon found that the maternity colony for these two bats was located in a dead elm tree in the old-growth woods of the biology preserve of Wright State University, less than two miles away, where they roosted with up to thirty-six other Indiana bats. The two bats with transmitters had a home range of up to 1,500 acres. The bats primarily foraged along the wooded Mad River corridor, but also over HPSNL.[9] This relationship between these two relatively small, isolated natural areas is a testament to the importance of conservation in a fragmented environment.

One of the animals that once inhabited the wet portions of the original Huffman Prairie is the eastern massasauga rattlesnake. This species is a resident of fens and wet prairies in the upper Midwest of the United States and Canada. Massasaugas are shy animals that feed on small mammals, other snakes, and invertebrates. While usually less than two feet long, their presence on Wright-Patterson Air Force Base has long been almost legendary. Since childhood, I have heard people say that golfers once had to push these snakes out of the way on the

Left: Eastern massasauga rattle-snake (*Sistrurus catenatus*). Photo by Gerald A. DeBoer/Shutterstock.com.

Below: TNC volunteer Greg Colwell with one of four eastern mas-sasauga rattlesnakes captured on Wright-Patterson Air Force Base in 1993. Photo by Terri Lucas.

golf greens with their putter, or claim that the base once brought in hogs to eat the snakes. John Van Cleve had found them on the prairie in the 1830s; there is no doubt that these little rattlers were common on Huffman Prairie before widespread drainage and development destroyed the fen and wet prairie habitat. As a result of the loss of this habitat, the State of Ohio now lists this species as endangered, and it

Right: Smooth green snake (*Opheodrys vernalis*) at HPSNL.

Below: DeKay's brown snake (*Storeria dekayi*) at HPSNL.

is under consideration for listing by the federal government.[10] A 1960 *Skywrighter* article tells of a massasauga found by a gardener near the base hospital under the leaves of a cucumber plant. It mentions "a big snake hunt, reminiscent of St. Patrick driving the reptiles from Ireland, drove off or killed most of our venomous enemies, but apparently, some of them escaped detection along the Mad River, and could be on the increase. A word of caution to gardeners, fishermen, hunters and those who like the great, snake-infested outdoors: 'Be careful!'"[11]

Because of the rarity of this species, Wright-Patterson conducts research to determine the status of this snake on the base. In July 1993, The Nature Conservancy volunteer Greg Colwell found four massasaugas southwest of the Huffman Prairie Flying Field. All of the snakes were captured and marked, and the two males were released. The females were pregnant and taken to the Dayton Museum of Natural History (now the Boonshoft Museum of Discovery), where the neonates, or baby snakes, were born. All of the young snakes were released back onto WPAFB property.[12] Since then, no massasaugas have been observed, despite a six-year study to locate them. As a result, this rare snake is now presumed to have been extirpated from Wright-Patterson.[13]

A silver lining of the unsuccessful effort to find massasaugas was the discovery of a significant population of smooth green snakes on the base, including HPSNL. These small, slender, bright green snakes of wet prairies were listed as endangered in Ohio in 2014 and had not

Larvae of tiger swallowtail (*Papilio glaucus*) at HPSNL.

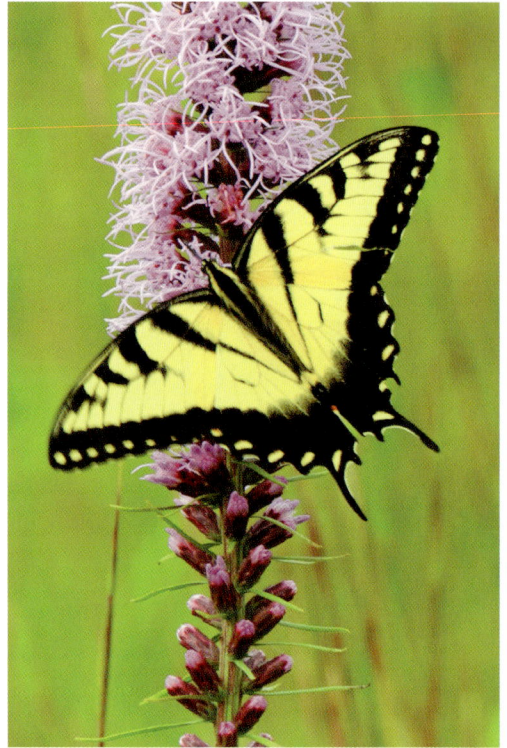

Adult tiger swallowtail on spiked blazing star (*Liatris spicata*). Photo by Tom Hissong.

been recorded in southwest Ohio in over fifty years.[14] This study also found healthy populations of DeKay's brown snakes and Eastern garter snakes on the prairie.[15]

Insects are by far the most diverse and numerous animals on HPSNL, but little is known about most of them. The first inventory of insects was a study of the lepidoptera (butterflies and moths) completed in 1992. This research documented 23 species of butterflies and 231 of moths. Subsequent research on moth populations identified twenty-eight species on HPSNL that were unknown in Ohio prior to this research, and three species new to science.[16] Much of the moth research was done by Eric Metzler, who named *Gnorimoschema huffmanellum* for Huffman Prairie and *Glyphidocera wrightorum* for the Wright brothers.[17] Five Rivers MetroParks and the Ohio Lepidopterists have conducted additional research on butterfly populations over the years, increasing the number of documented butterfly species to 38.

Management of lepidoptera is an important consideration for HPSNL. These creatures are dependent on the open character and unique vegetation of the site, which historically has been dependent on fire to maintain it. However, burning also can destroy overwintering eggs, larvae, and pupae of butterflies and moths, so care must be taken not to burn too much at one time.

Native bees are a common and important group of pollinating insects on the prairie. Bumblebees are abundant on HPSNL throughout the

Female tiger swallowtail at HPSNL.

Larvae of giant swallowtail (*Papilio cresphontes*) at HPSNL.

Adult giant swallowtail at HPSNL.

Pipevine swallowtail (*Battus philenor*) at HPSNL.

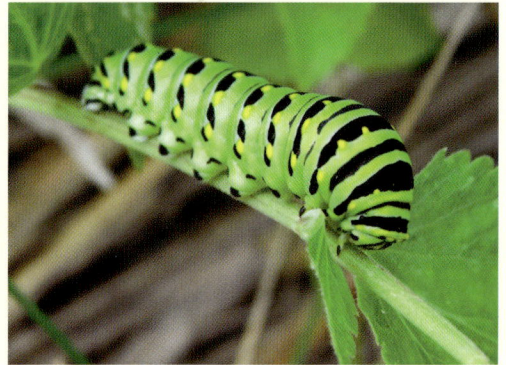

Black swallowtail (*Papilio polyxenes*) larvae at HPSNL.

Black swallowtail at HPSNL.

Variegated fritillary (*Euptoieta claudia*) at HPSNL.

Meadow fritillary (*Boloria bellona*) at HPSNL.

Monarch caterpillar (*Danaus plexippus*) on butterfly milkweed (*Asclepias tuberosa*) at HPSNL.

Above: Monarch on common milkweed (*Asclepias syriaca*) at HPSNL.

Left: Common buckeye (*Junonia coenia*). Photo by Tom Hissong.

Below: Eastern comma (*Polygonia comma*) at HPSNL.

American painted lady (*Vanessa virginiensis*) at HPSNL.

Red admiral (*Vanessa atalanta*) at HPSNL.

Eastern tailed blue (*Cupido comyntas*) at HPSNL.

Summer azure (*Celastrina neglecta*) at HPSNL.

Crossline skipper (*Polites origenes*) at HPSNL.

Pearl crescent (*Phyciodes tharos*) at HPSNL.

Hackberry emperor (*Asterocampa celtis*) at HPSNL.

Peck's skipper (*Polites peckius*) at HPSNL.

Left: Common checkered skipper (*Pyrgus communis*) at HPSNL.

Below: Silver-spotted skipper (*Epargyreus clarus*) at HPSNL.

Wild indigo duskywing (*Erynnis baptisiae*) at HPSNL.

Above: Clouded sulphur (*Colias philodice*) at HPSNL.

Left: Orange sulphur (*Colias eurytheme*) at HPSNL.

Plants and Animals of Huffman Prairie State Natural Landmark 121

Above: Cabbage whites (*Pieris rapae*) at HPSNL.

Above right: Virginia creeper sphinx moth (*Darapsa myron*) at HPSNL. Photo by Elisabeth Rothschild.

Right: Eight-spotted forester moth (*Alypia octomaculata*) at HPSNL. Photo by Elisabeth Rothschild.

Below: Elisabeth Rothschild documenting moths at HPSNL with the help of the Ohio Lepidopterists.

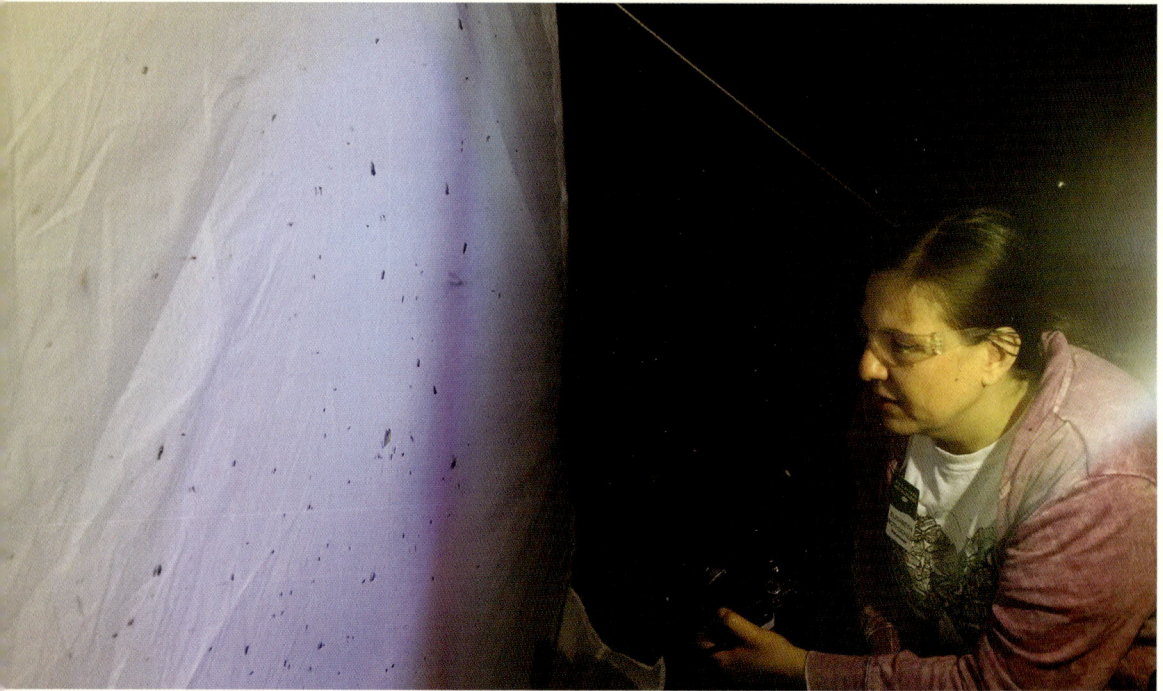

Delicate Cycnia (*Cycnia tenera*) at HPSNL.

Crambid snout moth (*Polygram-modes langdo-nalis*) at HPSNL. Photo by Elisabeth Rothschild.

Common Idia moth (*Idia ae-mula*) at HPSNL. Photo by Elisabeth Rothschild.

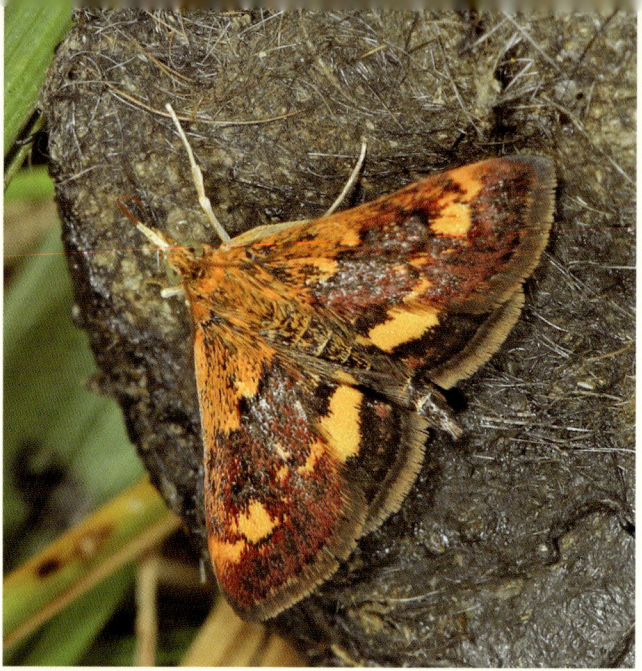

Orange-spotted pyrausta moth (*Pyrausta orphisalis*) at HPSNL. Photo by Jim McCormac.

Hummingbird clearwing (*Hemaris thysbe*) at HPSNL.

Above: Celery Looper (*Anagrapha falcifera*) at HPSNL.

Left: Larvae of clouded crimson moth (*Schinia gaurae*) on gaura (*Gaura biennis*) at HPSNL.

Above left: Bumblebee (*Bombus sp.*) and honey bee (*Apis cerana*) on common milkweed at HPSNL.

Above right: Sign for the Propolis Project east of Huffman Prairie Flying Field.

Left: Honey bees on a hive box, west of Huffman Prairie Flying Field.

growing season. Several species, including the common eastern bumble-bee, are continuously visiting flowers to obtain nectar and pollen. A recent arrival is the giant resin bee, a native of eastern Asia.[18]

An effort to help honey bees is happening west of the Huffman Prairie Flying Field. Here a group called the Propolis Project established four hives of honey bees in 2015. Propolis, funded by the Levin Family Foundation, is striving to establish local populations of honey bees that are resistant to varroa mites and can withstand Ohio winters.[19] Varroa mites feed on honey bees and their colonies and are reducing honey bee populations nationwide. While not native to Ohio or the United States, honey bees play an important role in pollinating fruit and vegetable crops.

Flower wasp (Family Thynnidae) at HPSNL.

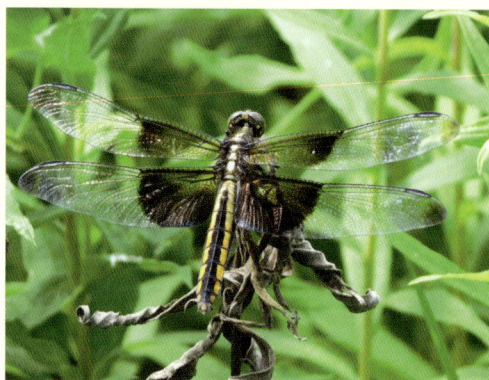
Female widow skimmer (*Libellula luctuosa*) at HPSNL.

Male widow skimmer at HPSNL.

Firefly in the genus *Ellychnia* at HPSNL.

Giant resin bees (*Megachile sculpturalis*) on butterfly milkweed at HPSNL.

Above left: Black blister beetle (*Epicauta pennsylvanica*) at HPSNL.

Above right: Dogbane beetle (*Chrysochus auratu*) at HPSNL.

Left: Giant robberfly (Genus *Promachus*) at HPSNL.

A large and undocumented diversity of insects from many families can be found on HPSNL in the summer. They often have strange and complicated life cycles and surprisingly beautiful colors and shapes.

Huffman Prairie, like all mesic prairies, has flora dominated by tall grasses and a wide variety of flowering plants, or forbs. The most common grasses are big bluestem, Indian grass, and little bluestem, with prairie cordgrass in low areas. The prairie is bright green, with lush clumps of these native grasses in June. Big bluestem starts to send up flowering stalks in July but blooms mainly in August. Its characteristic "turkey foot" flower stalks can reach over seven feet in wet years. Indian grass unfurls its flower stalks in August, peaking in September. Little bluestem also blooms in late summer but generally gets no taller than three feet. By the first frost in October each grass species takes on its own rich hue of fall color.

Above: Bush katydid (Genus *Scudderia*) at HPSNL.

Top right: Wheel bug nymph (*Arilus cristatus*) at HPSNL.

Bottom right: One of many grasshopper species at HPSNL.

Spring flowering plants include Canada anemone, Miami mist, Ohio spiderwort, black-eyed Susans, and butterfly milkweed, but in spring the prairie is mainly a lush growth of green.

The first big bloom peak is the third week of July. At that time HPSNL will boast gray-headed coneflower, purple coneflower, wild bergamot, royal catchfly, spike blazing star, prairie dock, whorled rosinweed, narrow-leaved mountain mint, and many others.

By mid-August the second wave of the flower show peaks, with field thistle, ironweed, Northern blazing star, and stiff goldenrod to name a few. September brings the sunflowers, which include six species on Huffman Prairie. The goldenrods and asters finish the floral show, starting in September and lasting until the first hard frost in October.

Nonnative plants are easily observed on HPSNL as well. Some, like smooth brome grass, nodding thistle, wild parsnip, poison hemlock, and white sweet clover are invasive species that are targeted for control. Others, like Queen Anne's lace, Deptford pink, and butter-and-eggs are not aggressive or a management concern.

Above: Indian grass (*Sorghastrum nutans*) at HPSNL.

Left: Big bluestem (*Andropogon gerardii*) at HPSNL.

Little bluestem (*Schizachyrium scoparium*) at HPSNL.

Prairie cordgrass (*Spartina pectinata*) at HPSNL.

Left: Wooly panic grass (*Dichanthelium clandestinum*) at HPSNL.

Below: Huffman Prairie State Natural Landmark has become a popular destination for botanists and nature lovers, particuarly in midsummer when the floral color reaches its peak.

Bottom: Each fall volunteers collect seed from Huffman Prairie State Natural Landmark for the ongoing prairie.

Smooth Solomon's seal (*Polygonatum biflorum*).
Photo by Roger Garber.

Northern adder's-tongue fern (*Ophioglossum pusillum*) at HPSNL.

Beaked corn salad (*Valerianella umbilicata*) with red admiral at HPSNL.

Tall meadow rue (*Thalictrum pubescens*) at HPSNL.

Canada anemone (*Anemone canadensis*) at HPSNL.

Miami mist (*Phacelia purshii*) and beaked corn salad (*Valerianella radiata*) at HPSNL.

Ohio spiderwort (*Tradescantia ohiensis*) at HPSNL.

Foxglove beard-tongue (*Penstemon digitalis*) at HPSNL.

Black-eyed Susan (*Rudbeckia hirta*) at HPSNL.

Butterfly milkweed (*Asclepias tuberosa*) at HPSNL.

Prairie rose (*Rosa setigera*) at HPSNL.

Common milkweed (*Asclepias syriaca*) at HPSNL.

Purple coneflower (*Echinacea purpurea*) at HPSNL.

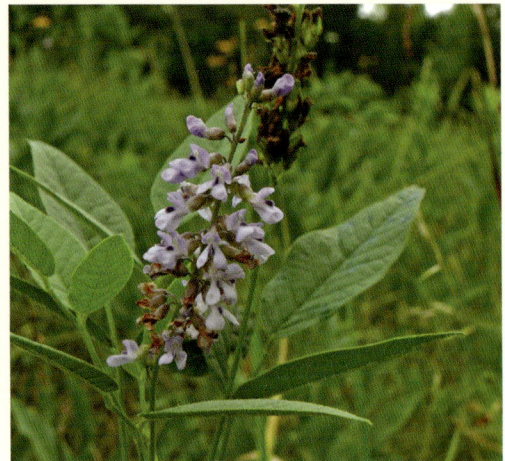

Wild petunia (*Ruellia humilis*) at HPSNL.

Scurf pea (*Orbexilum onobrychis*). Photo by Jim McCormac.

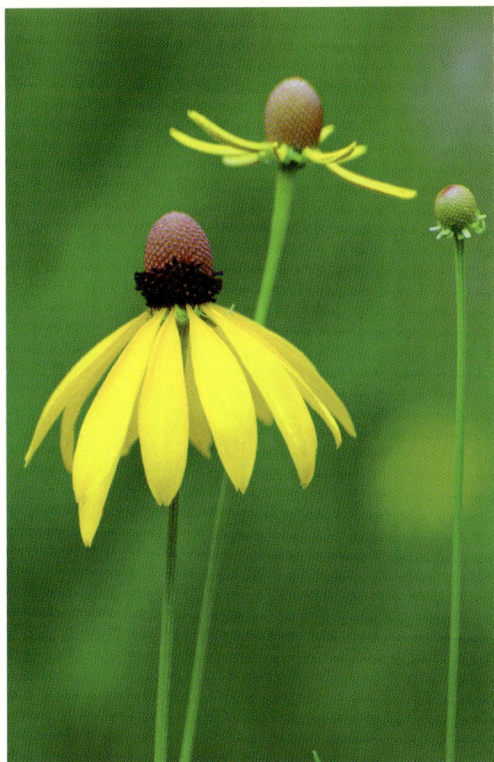

Gray-headed coneflower (*Ratibida pinnata*). Photo by Tom Hissong.

Royal catchfly (*Silene regia*) at HPSNL.

Wild bergamot (*Monarda fistulosa*) at HPSNL.

Prairie dock blossom at HPSNL.

Prairie dock (*Silphium terebinthinaceum*) at HPSNL.

White false indigo (*Baptisia alba*) at HPSNL.

Whorled rosinweed (*Silphium trifoliatum*) at HPSNL.

Three-leaved coneflower (*Rudbeckia triloba*) at HPSNL.

Culver's root (*Veronicastrum virginicum*) at HPSNL.

Glade mallow (*Napaea dioica*) at HPSNL.

Orange coneflower (*Rudbeckia fulgida*) at HPSNL.

Flowering spurge (*Euphorbia corollata*) at HPSNL.

Smooth oxeye (*Heliopsis helianthoides*) at HPSNL.

Right: Northern blazing star (*Liatris scariosa*) at HPSNL.

Below: Spiked blazing star (*Liatris spicata*) at HPSNL.

Jerusalem artichoke (*Helianthus tuberosa*) at HPSNL.

Hoary tick-trefoil (*Desmodium canescens*) at HPSNL.

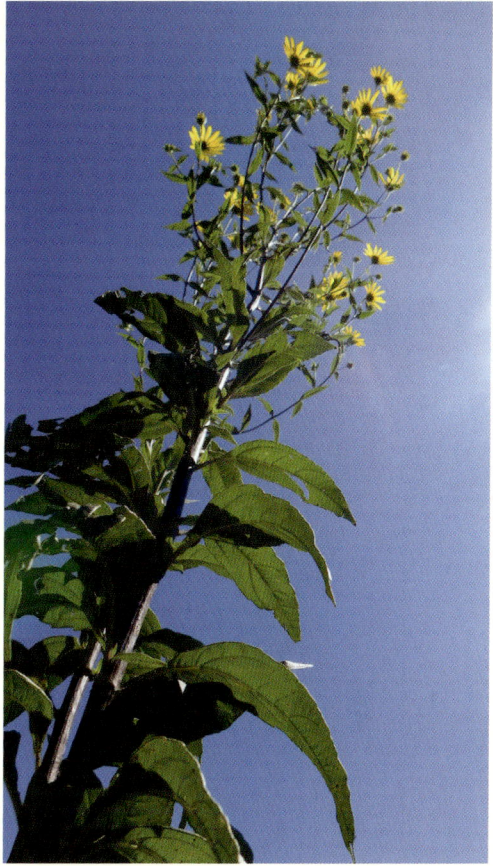

Above: Sawtooth sunflower (*Helianthus grosseserratus*) at HPSNL.

Below: Field thistle (*Cirsium discolor*) at HPSNL.

Tall ironweed (*Vernonia gigantea*) at HPSNL.

Southern wild senna (*Senna marilandica*) at HPSNL.

Hairy mountain-mint (*Pycnanthemum verticillatum*) at HPSNL.

Hollow-stemmed joe-pye weed (*Eutrochium fistulosum*) at HPSNL.

Potato vine (*Ipomoea pandurata*) at HPSNL.

Common ragweed (*Ambrosia artemisiifolia*) at HPSNL.

Obedient plant (*Physostegia virginiana*) at HPSNL.

Gaura (*Gaura biennis*) at HPSNL.

Stiff goldenrod (*Solidago rigida*). Photo by Tom Hissong.

Tall thoroughwort (*Eupatorium altissimum*) at HPSNL.

Above: New England aster (*Symphyotrichum novae-angliae*). Photo by Jim McCormac.

Left: Arrow-leaved aster (*Symphyotrichum urophyllum*) at HPSNL.

Nonnative smooth brome (*Bromus inermis*) at Huffman Prairie Flying Field.

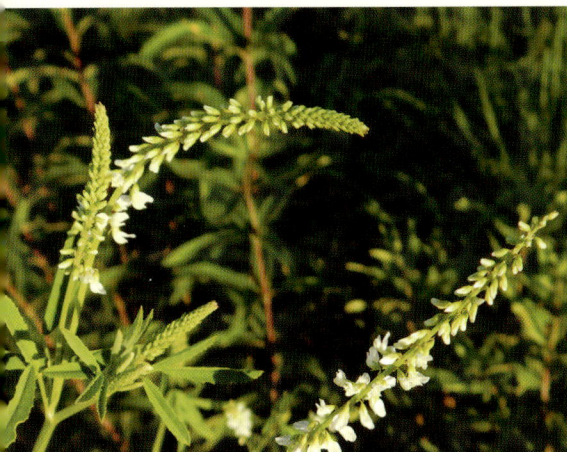

Nonnative poison hemlock (*Conium maculatum*) at HPSNL.

Nonnative white sweet clover (*Melilotus albus*) at HPSNL.

Nonnative wild parsnip (*Pastinaca sativa*) at HPSNL.

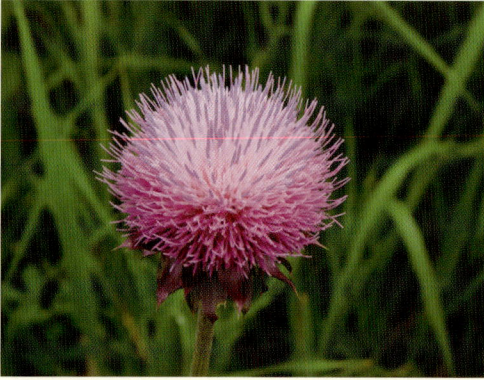

Nonnative nodding thistle (*Carduus nutans*) at HPSNL.

Nonnative Queen-Anne's lace (*Daucus carota*) at HPSNL.

Nonnative deptford pink (*Dianthus armeria*) at HPSNL.

Nonnative evening lychnis (*Silene latifolia*) at HPSNL.

Nonnative bladder campion (*Silene vulgaris*) at HPSNL.

Nonnative moth mullein (*Verbascum blattaria*) at HPSNL.

Nonnative butter and eggs (*Linaria vulgaris*) at HPSNL.

Dayton Aviation Heritage National Historical Park

When the Huffman Prairie State Natural Landmark was dedicated in 1986, the adjacent area, where the Wright brothers tested and flew the world's first practical powered aircraft, was a mown field without public access or significant recognition. In the 1940s, the air force had demolished the one remaining structure the Wrights had used, their 1910 hangar, from which they operated the Wright Flying School. Similarly, many of the other sites and buildings in the Dayton region pertaining to the Wright brothers were unprotected and without recognition.

The Huffman Prairie Flying Field is now an important part of a National Historical Park, visited by people from all over the world. Many people, agencies, and groups made this happen, but two people stand out as the driving force behind the interpretation and public recognition of the field and the creation of Dayton Aviation Heritage National Historical Park: Gerald Sharkey and Wilkinson Wright. Jerry knew the Dayton region was forgetting a vital part of its history. Along with others, he established Aviation Trail, Inc. in 1981; among its projects, the nonprofit organization created a brochure and self-guided tour of the various Dayton-area sites important to the Wright brothers and aviation history. In 1982, he discovered that two of the remaining buildings the Wrights had used, including one of their original bicycle shops, were scheduled for demolition. He lobbied for their preservation and purchased the bicycle shop for Aviation Trail with his own funds. Wilkinson Wright, a grandnephew of the inventors, joined the effort and became an effective spokesman, attending many meetings to build a consensus for the park's creation and advocating for the idea on a national level through his testimony to Congress and his work with officials of the National Park Service (NPS) officials.

In 1992, thanks in large measure to the efforts of these two men, President George H. W. Bush signed the bill that created Dayton Aviation Heritage National Historical Park. The park includes two NPS visitor centers and interprets six separate sites, each of which is an important piece of aviation history.

Entrance to Huffman Prairie Flying Field on Wright-Patterson Air Force Base.

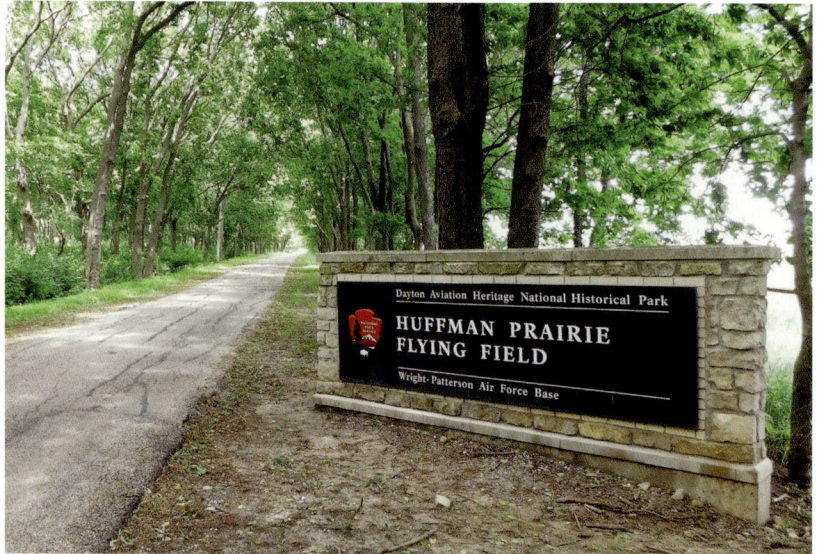

Huffman Prairie Flying Field, on Wright-Patterson Air Force Base, looks much the same as it did in 1904.

The Huffman Prairie Flying Field and Interpretive Center includes the Wright brothers' eighty-four-acre Huffman Prairie Flying Field (adjacent to the Huffman Prairie State Natural Landmark) and the Wright Memorial and Visitor Center on Wright Hill, one and one-half miles to the west.

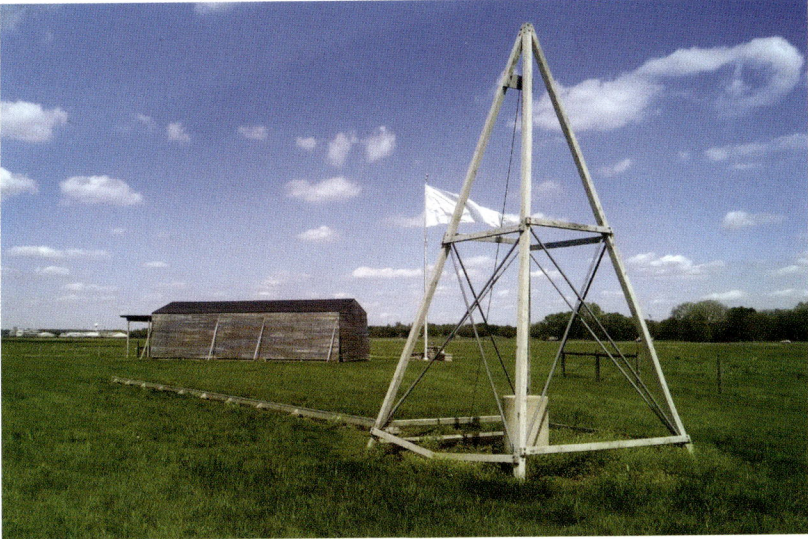

Left: Replicas of the 1905 hangar and launch system at Huffman Prairie Flying Field.

Below: National Park Service Ranger Adeseola Daboiku with Wright-B Flyer at the Huffman Prairie Flying Field, 2016.

Above: Displays inside the Huffman Prairie Flying Field Interpretive Center.

Right: Wright Memorial, adjacent to the Huffman Prairie Flying Field Interpretive Center.

Designating the pasture used by the Wrights as a National Historical Park site necessitated some changes to the security system at Wright-Patterson Air Force Base. Until then, any access to this site, or the adjacent Huffman Prairie State Natural Landmark, required visitors to first obtain a pass from the base security gate, a process that was not particularly easy. To solve this problem, WPAFB separated these sites from the more vital, active parts of Patterson Field and designated a public entrance route to the prairie from State Route 444.

The pasture the Wright brothers had used also posed a naming problem. "Huffman Prairie" had been used for the big patch of prairie along the Mad River at least since 1834, when John Leonard Riddell

Parking for
Huffman Prairie
State Natural Landmark

Parking for
Huffman Prairie
Flying Field
(National Park Service)

MARL RD.

Huffman
Prairie
State
Natural
Landmark

Huffman
Prairie
Flying
Field

PYLON RD.

HEBBLE CREEK RD.

Parking for
Rod and Gun Club

Twin Base Golf Course

COMMUNICATIONS BLVD

KAUFFMAN

MEMORIAL

Parking for
Twin Base
Golf Course

SR 444

Parking for
Huffman Prairie Flying
Field Interpretive Center
2380 Memorial Rd.
(National Park Service)

Gate 16a off SR 444
Entrance to WPAFB

DAYTON AVIATION HERITAGE
NATIONAL HISTORICAL PARK

Above: A map of the public facilities on Wright-Patterson Air Force Base near Huffman Prairie State Natural Landmark.

Left: Wright-Dunbar Interpretive Center, part of the Wright Cycle Company Complex at 16 South Williams Street in Dayton.

Wright Cycle Company Exhibit at the Wright Cycle Company Complex.

botanized there, but the adjacent Huffman Prairie State Natural Landmark, designated in 1986, already used that name. The NPS clarified things by naming the Wrights' space "Huffman Prairie Flying Field."

The flying field is directly west of the HPSNL and Pylon Road. The NPS has done an excellent job of interpreting the famous achievements that occurred there. The site includes replicas of the Wrights' 1905 hangar and of the rail and launch system used to boost the plane off the ground. The Park Service has also reconstructed the trolley platform that once stood at Simms Station, on the west side of the site. Regular programs and interpretive signs tell the rich story of the Wright brothers.

The Huffman Prairie Flying Field Visitor Center, at 2380 Memorial Road on WPAFB, features excellent displays, interpretive staff, and a gift shop. Next to the visitor center is the Wright Brothers Memorial, dedicated in 1940. For more information, call (937) 425-0008.

To visit the Huffman Prairie Flying Field or the Huffman Prairie State Natural Landmark, enter Wright-Patterson Air Force Base via gate 16-A, off SR 444. To visit the Huffman Prairie Flying Field Visitor Center and

Wright Memorial, enter Wright-Patterson Air Force Base from Memorial Road off Kauffman Avenue.

The Wright Cycle Company Complex in the Wrights' home neighborhood in West Dayton features the Wright-Dunbar Interpretive Center. The center contains two floors of impressive displays, the Aviation Trail Parachute Museum, and an excellent gift shop. The adjacent Wright Cycle Company exhibit is a restoration of one of the Wrights' bicycle shops.

Address: 16 South Williams Street, Dayton, Ohio 45402

Phone: (937) 225-7705.

The Paul Laurence Dunbar Historic Site in west Dayton, managed by Dayton History and owned by Ohio History Connection, preserves the home of well-known poet and friend of the Wrights, Paul Laurence Dunbar. The NPS conducts public tours of the site.

Address: 219 North Paul Laurence Dunbar Street, Dayton, OH 45402.

Phone: (937) 224-7061 or (937) 225-7705.

The Wright Brothers Aviation Center in Carillon Historical Park houses the world's first practical airplane, the 1905 Wright Flyer III, built by the Wright brothers and flown at Huffman Prairie. This aircraft is a National Historic Monument.

Paul Laurence Dunbar House, part of the Dayton Aviation Heritage National Historical Park, is located at 219 North Paul Laurence Dunbar St. in Dayton.

The 1905 Wright Flyer III at the Wright Brothers Aviation Center at Carillon Historical Park.

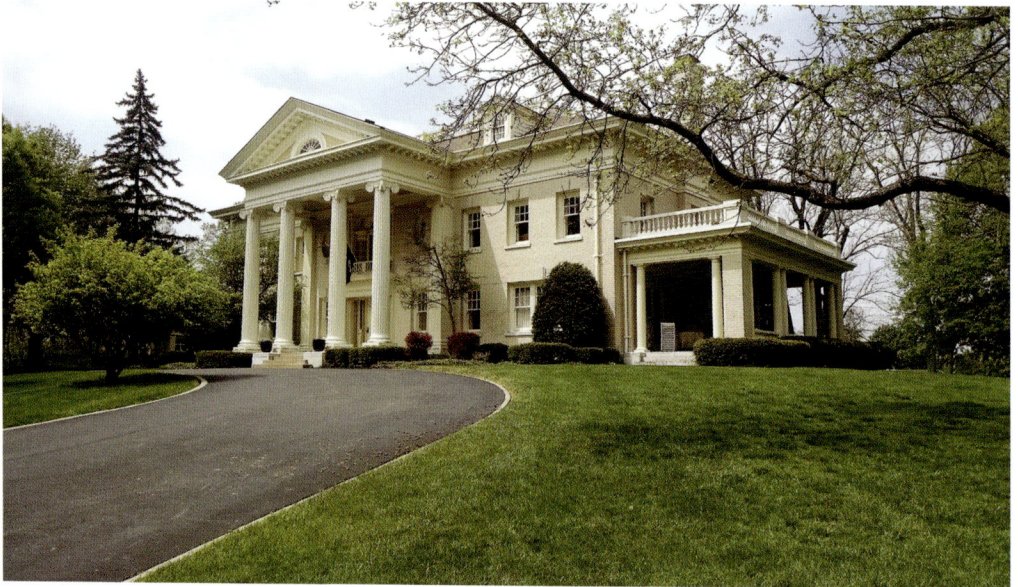

Hawthorn Hill, part of the Dayton Aviation Heritage National Historical Park, was home to Orville Wright from 1914 until his death in 1948.

Address: 1000 Carillon Boulevard, Dayton, OH 45409

Phone: (937) 293-2841

Hawthorn Hill, a National Historic Landmark in Oakwood, is the mansion the Wrights designed and was Orville's home for many years. Tours can be arranged through Dayton History by calling (937) 293-2841.

The Wright Company Factory site, still privately owned and not yet open to the public, also in West Dayton, includes the world's first airplane factory.

Flora Documented on Huffman
Prairie State Natural Landmark

1. Ohio COC, or Coefficient of Conservatism. A measure (0–10) of the ecological tolerances of plant species, with 0 representing species with a wide range of tolerance such as common ragweed (*Ambrosia artemisiifolia*), and 10 being a species with a narrow range of ecological tolerances such as showy lady's slipper orchid (*Cypripedium reginae*), from Andreas, Mack, and McCormac, http://www.epa.ohio.gov/portals/35/wetlands/Ohio_FQAI.pdf.

2. Ohio Prairie Indicator. Plant species characteristic of the presettlement prairies of Ohio, from Ohio Prairie Association, http://www.ohioprairie.org/page110.html.

3. Origin of plant species of Huffman Prairie. Native species are those that are native to Ohio, alien species are native elsewhere but are now present in the local flora, from United States Department of Agriculture, Natural Resources Conservation Service Plants Database (http://plants.usda.gov).

4. Source of plant species found on Huffman Prairie State Natural Landmark, from records of David Nolin. 1=found on site without intentional introduction, 2=reintroduced from seed or plugs as part of restoration effort, 3=found on site naturally *and* planted from seed or plugs, 4=native species that returned since 1986 without intentional reintroduction.

Type	Family	Scientific Name	Common Name	Ohio COC[1]	Ohio Prairie Indicator[2]	Class[3]	Source[4]
forb/herb	Euphorbiaceae	Acalypha rhomboidea	rhombic three-seed mercury	0		native	1
tree	Aceraceae	Acer negundo	box elder	3		native	1
tree	Aceraceae	Acer saccharinum	silver maple	3		native	1
forb/herb	Asteraceae	Achillea millefolium	yarrow	1		native	1
forb/herb	Scrophulariaceae	Agalinis tenuifolia	slender foxglove	4	X	native	4
forb/herb	Asteraceae	Ageratina altissima	white snakeroot	3		native	1
graminoid	Poaceae	Agropyron repens	quackgrass	0		alien	0
graminoid	Poaceae	Agrostis gigantea	redtop	0		alien	0
tree	Simaroubaceae	Ailanthus altissima	tree-of-heaven	0		alien	0
forb/herb	Brassicaceae	Alliaria petiolata	garlic mustard	0		alien	0
forb/herb	Liliaceae	Allium canadense	wild garlic	2	X	native	1
forb/herb	Liliaceae	Allium cernuum	nodding wild onion	5	X	native	3
forb/herb	Liliaceae	Allium vineale	field garlic	0		alien	0
forb/herb	Amaranthaceae	Amaranthus albus	tumbleweed	0		native	1
forb/herb	Amaranthaceae	Amaranthus retroflexus	redroot	0		alien	0
forb/herb	Asteraceae	Ambrosia artemisiifolia	common ragweed	0		native	1
forb/herb	Asteraceae	Ambrosia trifida	giant ragweed	0		native	1
graminoid	Poaceae	Andropogon gerardii	big bluestem	5	X	native	3
graminoid	Poaceae	Andropogon virginicus	common broom-sedge	3		native	1
forb/herb	Ranunculaceae	Anemone canadensis	Canada anemone	5	X	native	1
forb/herb	Ranunculaceae	Anemone virginiana	woodland thimbleweed	3	X	native	4
forb/herb	Compositae	Antennaria plantaginia	plantain-leaved pussy-toes	1	X	native	4
forb/herb	Apocynaceae	Apocynum cannabinum	Indian hemp	1	X	native	1

forb/herb	Asteraceae	*Arctium minus*	common burdock	0		alien	0
graminoid	Caryophyllaceae	*Arenaria serpyllifolia*	thyme-leaved sandwort	0		alien	0
forb/herb	Poaceae	*Aristida oligantha*	plains three-awned grass	1		native	1
forb/herb	Asteraceae	*Arnoglossum atriplicifolium*	pale Indian-plantain	6	X	native	1
forb/herb	Asclepiadaceae	*Asclepias syriaca*	common milkweed	1		native	1
forb/herb	Asclepiadaceae	*Asclepias tuberosa*	butterfly-weed	4	X	native	1
forb/herb	Asparagaceae	*Asparagus officinalis*	asparagus	0		alien	0
forb/herb	Aspleniaceae	*Asplenium platyneuron*	ebony spleenwort	3		native	1
forb/herb	Fabaceae	*Baptisia australis*	blue false indigo	6	X	native	2
forb/herb	Fabaceae	*Baptisia lactea*	white false indigo	8	X	native	2
forb/herb	Brassicaceae	*Barbarea verna*	early winter cress	0		alien	0
forb/herb	Asteraceae	*Bidens aristosa*	Midwest tickseed-sunflower	4	X	native	4
forb/herb	Asteraceae	*Bidens vulgata*	tall beggar's-ticks	2	X	native	4
forb/herb	Lamiaceae	*Blephilia ciliata*	downy woodmint	4	X	native	3
forb/herb	Brassicaceae	*Brassica nigra*	black mustard	0		alien	0
forb/herb	Asteraceae	*Brickellia eupatorioides*	false boneset	7	X	native	2
graminoid	Poaceae	*Bromus commutatus*	hairy chess	0		alien	0
graminoid	Poaceae	*Bromus inermis*	Hungarian brome	0		alien	0
graminoid	Poaceae	*Bromus japonicus/arvensis*	Japanese brome	0		alien	0
forb/herb	Poaceae	*Bromus tectorum*	downy brome	0		alien	0
forb/herb	Boraginaceae	*Buglossoides arvensis*	corn gromwell	0		alien	0
vine	Convolvulaceae	*Calystegia sepium*	hedge bindweed	1		native	1
vine	Bignoniaceae	*Campsis radicans*	trumpet-creeper	1		native	1
forb/herb	Brassicaceae	*Capsella bursa-pastoris*	sheherd's purse	0		alien	0

Type	Family	Scientific Name	Common Name	Ohio COC[1]	Ohio Prairie Indicator[2]	Class[3]	Source[4]
forb/herb	Brassicaceae	*Cardamine hirsuta*	hoary bitter-cress	0		alien	0
forb/herb	Asteraceae	*Carduus nutans*	nodding thistle	0		alien	0
graminoid	Cyperaceae	*Carex amphibola*	eastern narrow-leaved sedge	5		native	1
graminoid	Cyperaceae	*Carex blanda*	common wood sedge	1		native	1
graminoid	Cyperaceae	*Carex brevior*	tufted-fescue sedge	8	X	native	1
graminoid	Cyperaceae	*Carex davisii*	Davis' sedge	5		native	1
graminoid	Cyperaceae	*Carex festucacea*	fescue sedge	8	X	native	1
graminoid	Cyperaceae	*Carex granularis*	meadow sedge	3		native	1
graminoid	Cyperaceae	*Carex leavenworthii*	Leavenworth's sedge	3		native	1
graminoid	Cyperaceae	*Carex molesta*	troublesome sedge	3		native	1
graminoid	Cyperaceae	*Carex retroflexa*	reflexed sedge	4		native	1
tree	Ulmaceae	*Celtis occidentalis*	hackberry	4		native	1
forb/herb	Caryophyllaceae	*Cerastium vulgatum*	common chickweed	0		alien	0
forb/herb	Euphorbiaceae	*Chamaesyce maculata*	milk purslane	0		native	1
forb/herb	Amaranthaceae	*Chenopodium album*	lambs quarters	0		alien	0
forb/herb	Amaranthaceae	*Chenopodium berlanderii*	pitted goosefoot	1		native	1
forb/herb	Asteraceae	*Cichorium intybus*	chicory	0		alien	0
forb/herb	Asteraceae	*Cirsium arvense*	Canada thistle	0		alien	0
forb/herb	Asteraceae	*Cirsium discolor*	field thistle	4	X	native	1
forb/herb	Asteraceae	*Cirsium muticum*	swamp thistle	8	X	native	2
vine	Ranunculaceae	*Clematis virginiana*	virgin's bower	3		native	1
forb/herb	Apiaceae	*Conium maculatum*	poison-hemlock	0		alien	0
forb/herb	Asteraceae	*Conoclinium coelestinum*	mistflower	3		native	2

vine	Convolvulaceae	*Convolvulus arvensis*	field bindweed	0		native	1
forb/herb	Asteraceae	*Conyza canadensis*	horseweed	0		native	1
forb/herb	Compositae	*Coreopsis tripteris*	tall tickseed	5	X	native	2
shrub	Cornaceae	*Cornus racemosa*	gray dogwood	1	X	native	1
forb/herb	Rubiaceae	*Cruciata pedemontana*	piedmont bedstraw	0		alien	0
vine	Asclepiadaceae	*Cynanchum laeve*	sand-vine	1		native	1
graminoid	Cyperaceae	*Cyperus esculentus*	yellow nut-sedge	0		native	1
graminoid	Poaceae	*Dactylis glomerata*	orchard grass	0		alien	0
forb/herb	Solanaceae	*Datura stramonium*	jimsonweed	0		native	1
forb/herb	Apiaceae	*Daucus carota*	Queen-Anne's lace	0		alien	0
forb/herb	Brassicaceae	*Descurainia pinnata*	tansy-mustard	8	X	native	4
forb/herb	Fabaceae	*Desmodium canescens*	hoary tick-trefoil	4	X	native	1
forb/herb	Caryophyllaceae	*Dianthus armeria*	Deptford-pink	0		alien	0
graminoid	Poaceae	*Dichanthelium acuminatum*	Woolly panic grass	3	X	native	1
graminoid	Poaceae	*Dichanthelium clandestinum*	deers-tongue panic grass	2		native	1
graminoid	Poaceae	*Dichanthelium sabulorum*	hemlock rosette grass	3		native	1
graminoid	Poaceae	*Digitaria sanguinalis*	northern crabgrass	0		alien	0
forb/herb	Dioscoreaceae	*Dioscorea villosa*	wild yam	5		native	1
forb/herb	Dipsacaceae	*Dipsacus laciniatus*	cut-leaved teasel	0		alien	0
forb/herb	Dipsacaceae	*Dipsacus sylvestris*	wild teasel	0		alien	0
forb/herb	Brassicaceae	*Draba verna*	whitlow-grass	0		alien	0
forb/herb	Asteraceae	*Echinacea purpurea*	purple coneflower	6	X	native	2
graminoid	Poaceae	*Echinochloa muricata*	rough barnyard grass	0		alien	0
shrub	Elaeagnaceae	*Elaeagnus umbellata*	autumn-olive	0		alien	0
graminoid	Poaceae	*Eleusine indica*	goose grass	0		alien	0

Type	Family	Scientific Name	Common Name	Ohio COC[1]	Ohio Prairie Indicator[2]	Class[3]	Source[4]
graminoid	Poaceae	*Elymus canadensis*	Canada wild rye	6	X	native	2
fern	Equisetaceae	*Equisetum arvense*	field horsetail	0		native	1
graminoid	Poaceae	*Eragrostis capillaris*	lace grass	3		native	1
graminoid	Poaceae	*Eragrostis minor*	low love grass	0		alien	0
graminoid	Poaceae	*Eragrostis spectabilis*	purple love grass	2	X	native	1
forb/herb	Asteraceae	*Erechtites hieraciifolia*	pilewort	2		native	1
forb/herb	Asteraceae	*Erigeron annuus*	daisy fleabane	0		native	1
forb/herb	Asteraceae	*Erigeron philadelphicus*	Philadelphia fleabane	2		native	1
forb/herb	Asteraceae	*Erigeron strigosus*	rough fleabane	1		native	1
forb/herb	Apiaceae	*Eryngium yuccifolium*	rattlesnake master	7	X	native	2
forb/herb	Asteraceae	*Eupatorium altissimum*	tall thoroughwort	0	X	native	1
forb/herb	Asteraceae	*Eupatorium serotinum*	late flowering boneset	2		native	4
forb/herb	Euphorbiaceae	*Euphorbia corollata*	flowering spurge	4	X	native	1
forb/herb	Euphorbiaceae	*Euphorbia dentata*	toothed spurge	0		native	1
forb/herb	Asteraceae	*Euthamia graminifolia*	flat-topped goldenrod	2	X	native	1
forb/herb	Asteraceae	*Eutrochium fistulosum*	hollow-stemmed joe-pye weed	6		native	2
forb/herb	Asteraceae	*Eutrochium maculatum*	spotted joe-pye weed	5	X	native	2
forb/herb	Roseaceae	*Fragaria virginiana*	wild strawberry	1		native	1
tree	Oleaceae	*Fraxinus nigra*	black ash	7		native	1
tree	Oleaceae	*Fraxinus pennsylvanica*	green ash	3		native	1
forb/herb	Rubiaceae	*Galium aparine*	cleavers	0	X	native	1
forb/herb	Rubiaceae	*Galium mollugo*	white bedstraw	0		alien	0
forb/herb	Onagraceae	*Gaura biennis*	gaura	1	X	native	1

Growth form	Family	Scientific name	Common name			Status	
forb/herb	Geraniaceae	*Geranium pusillum*	small-flowered crane's-bill	0		alien	0
forb/herb	Rosaceae	*Geum canadense*	white avens	2		native	4
forb/herb	Lamiaceae	*Glechoma hederacea*	ground ivy	0		alien	0
tree	Fabaceae	*Gleditsia triacanthos*	honey locust	4		native	1
forb/herb	Boraginaceae	*Hackelia virginica*	Virginia stickseed	2		native	1
forb/herb	Asteraceae	*Helianthus giganteus*	swamp sunflower	6	X	native	1
forb/herb	Asteraceae	*Helianthus grosseseratus*	sawtooth sunflower	4	X	native	2
forb/herb	Asteraceae	*Helianthus hirsutus*	hairy sunflower	4		native	1
forb/herb	Asteraceae	*Helianthus maximiliani*	Maximilian sunflower	0	X	native	2
forb/herb	Asteraceae	*Helianthus mollis*	ashy sunflower	7	X	native	2
forb/herb	Asteraceae	*Helianthus tuberosus*	Jerusalem-artichoke	3		native	1
forb/herb	Asteraceae	*Heliopsis helianthoides*	smooth oxeye	5	X	native	3
forb/herb	Liliaceae	*Hemerocallis fulva*	orange day-lily	0		alien	0
forb/herb	Brassicaceae	*Hesperis matronalis*	dames rocket	0		alien	0
forb/herb	Malvaceae	*Hibiscus trionum*	flower-of-an-hour	0		alien	0
vine	Cannabaceae	*Humulus lupulus*	common hops	2		native	1
forb/herb	Hyperacaceae	*Hypericum punctatum*	spotted St. Johns-wort	2		native	1
vine	Convolvulaceae	*Ipomoea pandurata*	potato-vine	2	X	native	1
tree	Cuppressaceae	*Juniperus virginiana*	eastern red cedar	3		native	1
forb/herb	Asteraceae	*Lactuca canadensis*	wild lettuce	1	X	native	1
forb/herb	Asteraceae	*Lactuca saligna*	willow-leaved lettuce	0		alien	0
forb/herb	Asteraceae	*Lactuca serriola*	prickly lettuce	0		alien	0
forb/herb	Lamiaceae	*Lamium amplexicaule*	henbit	0		alien	0
forb/herb	Lamiaceae	*Lamium purpureum*	purple dead-nettle	0		alien	0
forb/herb	Lamiaceae	*Leonurus cardiaca*	motherwort	0		alien	0

Type	Family	Scientific Name	Common Name	Ohio COC[1]	Ohio Prairie Indicator[2]	Class[3]	Source[4]
forb/herb	Brassicaceae	*Lepidium campestre*	field peppergrass	0		alien	0
forb/herb	Asteraceae	*Leucanthemum vulgare*	ox-eye daisy	0		alien	0
forb/herb	Scrophulariaceae	*Leucospora multifida*	leucospora	5		native	4
forb/herb	Asteraceae	*Liatris scariosa*	northern blazing star	6	X	native	2
forb/herb	Asteraceae	*Liatris spicata*	spiked blazing star	7	X	native	3
forb/herb	Scrophulariaceae	*Linaria vulgaris*	butter-and-eggs	0		alien	0
forb/herb	Campanulaceae	*Lobelia inflata*	Indian-tobacco	1		native	1
forb/herb	Campanulaceae	*Lobelia spicata*	pale-spike lobelia	5	X	native	4
vine	Caprifoliaceae	*Lonicera japonica*	Japanese honeysuckle	0		alien	0
shrub	Caprifoliaceae	*Lonicera maackii*	Amur honeysuckle	0		alien	0
forb/herb	Lamiaceae	*Lycopus americana*	American water-horehound	3	X	native	4
forb/herb	Primulaceae	*Lysimachia ciliata*	fringed loosestrife	4		alien	0
tree	Moraceae	*Maclura pomifera*	osage-orange	0		alien	0
forb/herb	Malvaceae	*Malva neglecta*	cheese mallow	0		alien	0
forb/herb	Fabaceae	*Medicago lupulina*	black medick	0		alien	0
forb/herb	Fabaceae	*Medicago sativa*	alfalfa	0		alien	0
forb/herb	Fabaceae	*Melilotus alba*	white sweet-clover	0		alien	0
forb/herb	Fabaceae	*Melilotus officinalis*	yellow sweet-clover	0		alien	0
forb/herb	Menispermaceae	*Menispermum canadense*	Canada moonseed	5		native	1
forb/herb	Lamiaceae	*Mentha arvensis*	field mint	2		native	1
forb/herb	Brassicaceae	*Microthlaspi perfoliatum*	claspleaf pennycress	0		alien	0
forb/herb	Nyctaginaceae	*Mirabilis nyctaginea*	Heart-leaved four-o'clock	0	X	native	1
forb/herb	Molluginaceae	*Mollugo verticillata*	carpet-weed	0		native	1

forb/herb	Lamiaceae	*Monarda fistulosa*	wild bergamot	3	X	native	3
tree	Moraceae	*Morus alba*	white mulberry	0		alien	0
graminoid	Poaceae	*Muhlenbergia frondosa*	common satin grass	3		native	1
graminoid	Poaceae	*Muhlenbergia schreberi*	nimblewill	0		native	1
forb/herb	Caryophyllaceae	*Myoston aquaticum*	giant chickweed	0		alien	0
forb/herb	Malvaceae	*Napaea dioica*	glade-mallow	4		native	1
forb/herb	Lamiaceae	*Nepeta cataria*	catnip	0		alien	0
forb/herb	Onagraceae	*Oenothera biennis*	common evening-primrose	1		native	1
forb/herb	Asteraceae	*Oligoneuron rigida*	stiff goldenrod	8	X	native	2
forb/herb	Boraginaceae	*Onosmodium bejariense*	false gromwell	7	X	native	2
forb/herb	Ophioglossaceae	*Ophioglossum pucillum*	northern adder's-tongue	6		native	4
forb/herb	Fabaceae	*Orbexilum onobrychis*	scurf pea	5	X	native	4
forb/herb	Oxalidaceae	*Oxalis corniculata*	creeping wood-sorrel	0		alien	0
forb/herb	Oxalidaceae	*Oxalis stricta*	common yellow wood-sorrel	0		native	1
graminoid	Asteraceae	*Packera aurea*	golden ragwort	4	X	native	4
forb/herb	Asteraceae	*Packera glabella*	butterweed	0		native	1
graminoid	Poaceae	*Panicum capillare*	witch grass	1		native	1
graminoid	Poaceae	*Panicum virgatum*	switch grass	4	X	native	2
vine	Vitaceae	*Parthenocissus inserta*	Virginia creeper	2		native	1
graminoid	Poaceae	*Paspalum pubiflorum*	hairy-flowered papsalum	3		native	1
graminoid	Poaceae	*Paspalum setaceum*	thin paspalum	2		native	1
forb/herb	Apiaceae	*Pastinaca sativa*	wild parsnip	0		alien	0
forb/herb	Scrophulariaceae	*Penstemon digitalis*	foxglove beard-tongue	2	X	native	3
forb/herb	Scrophulariaceae	*Penstemon hirsutus*	hairy beard-tongue	3	X	native	1
forb/herb	Hydrophyllaceae	*Phacelia purshii*	miami-mist	4		native	1

Type	Family	Scientific Name	Common Name	Ohio COC[1]	Ohio Prairie Indicator[2]	Class[3]	Source[4]
graminoid	Poaceae	Phleum pratense	timothy	0		alien	0
forb/herb	Solanaceae	Physalis heterophylla	clammy ground-cherry	1		native	1
forb/herb	Solanaceae	Physalis longifolia	smooth ground-cherry	1		native	1
forb/herb	Lamiaceae	Physostegia virginiana	obedient plant	5	X	native	2
forb/herb	Phytolaccaceae	Phytolacca americana	pokeweed	1		native	1
forb/herb	Plantaginaceae	Plantago lanceolata	English plantain	0		alien	0
forb/herb	Orchidaceae	Platanthera lacera	ragged fringed orchid	3		native	1
graminoid	Poaceae	Poa compressa	Canada bluegrass	0		alien	0
graminoid	Poaceae	Poa pratensis	Kentucky bluegrass	0		alien	0
forb/herb	Polygalaceae	Polygala verticillata	whorled milkwort	2	X	native	4
forb/herb	Liliaceae	Polygonatum biflorum	smooth Solomon's-seal	4	X	native	4
forb/herb	Polygonaceae	Polygonum amphibian	water smartweed	4	X	native	1
vine	Polygonaceae	Polygonum convovulus	black bindweed	0		alien	0
vine	Polygonaceae	Polygonum pensylvanicum	pinkweed	0		native	1
vine	Salicaceae	Polygonum scandens	climbing false buckwheat	2		native	1
tree	Portulacaceae	Populus deltoides	Eastern cottonwood	3		native	1
forb/herb	Rosaceae	Portulaca oleracea	common purslane	0		alien	0
forb/herb	Rosaceae	Potentilla norvegica	strawberry-weed	1		native	1
forb/herb	Lamiaceae	Potentilla recta	rough-fruited cinquefoil	0		alien	0
forb/herb	Rosaceae	Prunella vulgaris	self-heal	0		native	1
tree	Rosaceae	Prunus americana	wild plum	3	X	native	1
tree	Asteraceae	Prunus serotina	black cherry	3		native	1
forb/herb	Rutaceae	Pseudognaphalium obtusifolium	fragrant cudweed	2	X	native	4

Growth form	Family	Scientific name	Common name				
shrub	Lamiaceae	*Ptelea trifoliata*	hop-tree	5		native	1
forb/herb	Lamiaceae	*Pycnanthemum tenuifolium*	narrow-leaved mountain-mint	4	X	native	2
forb/herb	Lamiaceae	*Pycnanthemum verticillatum*	hairy mountain-mint	5		native	2
forb/herb	Lamiaceae	*Pycnanthemum viginianum*	Virginia mountain-mint	4	X	native	2
tree	Rosaceae	*Pyrus calleryana*	callery pear	0		alien	0
forb/herb	Asteraceae	*Ranunculus abortivus*	kidney-leaved buttercup	1	X	native	1
forb/herb	Rhamnaceae	*Ratibida pinnata*	gray-headed coneflower	5	X	native	3
tree	Anacardiaceae	*Rhamnus cathartica*	European buckthorn	0		alien	0
shrub	Rosaceae	*Rhus glabra*	smooth sumac	2		native	2
shrub	Rosaceae	*Rosa carolina*	pasture rose	4	X	native	1
shrub	Rosaceae	*Rosa setigera*	climbing prarie rose	4		native	1
shrub	Rosaceae	*Rubus allegheniensis*	common blackberry	1	X	native	4
shrub	Rosaceae	*Rubus flagellaris*	northern dewberry	1		native	1
shrub	Rosaceae	*Rubus occidentalis*	black raspberry	1	X	native	1
shrub	Rosaceae	*Rubus pensilvanicus*	Pennsylvania blackberry	1		native	1
forb/herb	Asteraceae	*Rudbeckia fulgida*	orange coneflower	6	X	native	2
forb/herb	Asteraceae	*Rudbeckia hirta*	black-eyed Susan	1	X	native	3
forb/herb	Asteraceae	*Rudbeckia laciniata*	green-headed coneflower	6		native	1
forb/herb	Asteraceae	*Rudbeckia triloba*	three-lobed coneflower	5	X	native	1
forb/herb	Acanthaceae	*Ruellia humilis*	wild petunia	6	X	native	1
forb/herb	Polygonaceae	*Rumex acetosella*	sheep sorrel	0		alien	0
forb/herb	Polygonaceae	*Rumex crispus*	curly dock	0		alien	0
forb/herb	Gentianaceae	*Sabatia angularis*	rose-pink	4	X	native	1
tree	Salicaceae	*Salix exigua*	sandbar willow	1		native	1
shrub	Caprifoliaceae	*Sambucus canadensis*	common elderberry	3		native	1

Type	Family	Scientific Name	Common Name	Ohio COC[1]	Ohio Prairie Indicator[2]	Class[3]	Source[4]
forb/herb	Caryophyllaceae	Saponaria officinalis	soapwort	0		alien	0
graminoid	Poaceae	Schedonorus pratensis	meadow fescue	0		alien	0
graminoid	Poaceae	Schizachyrium scoparium	little bluestem	5	X	native	1
forb/herb	Fabaceae	Securigera varia	crown-vetch	0		alien	0
forb/herb	Fabaceae	Senna hebecarpa	northern wild senna	4	X	native	2
forb/herb	Fabaceae	Senna marilandica	Maryland wild senna	4	X	native	2
graminoid	Poaceae	Setaria faberi	giant foxtail grass	0		alien	0
graminoid	Poaceae	Setaria glauca	yellow foxtail grass	0		alien	0
forb/herb	Cucurbitaceae	Sicyos angulatus	bur-cucumber	3		native	1
forb/herb	Caryophyllaceae	Silene antirrhina	sleepy catchfly	1		native	1
forb/herb	Caryophyllaceae	Silene latifolia	white campion	0		alien	0
forb/herb	Caryophyllaceae	Silene regia	royal catchfly	8	X	native	2
forb/herb	Asteraceae	Silphium perfoliatum	cup-plant	6	X	native	1
forb/herb	Asteraceae	Silphium terebinthinaceum	prairie dock	8	X	native	2
forb/herb	Asteraceae	Silphium trifoliatum	whorled rosin-weed	5	X	native	2
forb/herb	Iridaceae	Sisyrinchium angustifolium	stout blue-eyed grass	2	X	native	1
vine	Smilacaceae	Smilax herbacea	carrion flower	4		native	4
forb/herb	Solonaceae	Solanum carolinense	horse nettle	0	X	native	1
forb/herb	Solanaceae	Solanum nigrum	black nightshade	0		alien	0
forb/herb	Asteraceae	Solidago altissima	tall goldenrod	1		native	1
graminoid	Poaceae	Sorghastrum nutans	Indian grass	5	X	native	3
graminoid	Poaceae	Sorghum halepense	Johnson grass	0		alien	0
graminoid	Poaceae	Spartina pectinata	prairie cord grass	5	X	native	1

forb/herb	Orchidaceae	*Spiranthes ovalis*	slender ladies'-tresses	6		native	4
graminoid	Poaceae	*Sporobolis heterolepsis*	prairie dropseed	8	X	native	2
graminoid	Poaceae	*Sporobolus asper*	tall dropseed	2	X	native	1
forb/herb	Caryophyllaceae	*Stellaria graminea*	common stitchwort	0		alien	0
forb/herb	Caryophyllaceae	*Stellaria media*	common chickweed	0		alien	0
forb/herb	Asteraceae	*Symphyotrichum laeve*	smooth aster	6	X	native	4
forb/herb	Asteraceae	*Symphyotrichum lateriflorum*	calico aster	2		native	1
forb/herb	Asteraceae	*Symphyotrichum novae-angliae*	New England aster	2	X	native	1
forb/herb	Asteraceae	*Symphyotrichum pilosum*	awl aster	1		native	1
forb/herb	Asteraceae	*Symphyotrichum racemosum*	small-headed aster	2		native	1
forb/herb	Asteraceae	*Symphytrichum lanceolatum*	Eastern lined aster	3		native	1
forb/herb	Asteraceae	*Symphyotrichum urophyllum*	arrow-leaved aster	3		native	4
forb/herb	Asteraceae	*Taraxacum officinale*	common dandelion	0		alien	0
forb/herb	Lamiaceae	*Teucrium canadense*	American germander	3	X	native	1
forb/herb	Ranunculaceae	*Thalictrum pubsecens*	tall meadow rue	5		native	1
forb/herb	Brassicaceae	*Thlaspi arvense*	field penny cress	0		alien	0
vine	Anacardiaceae	*Toxicodendron radicans*	poison-ivy	1		native	1
forb/herb	Commelinaceae	*Tradescantia ohiensis*	Ohio spiderwort	5	X	native	2
forb/herb	Asteraceae	*Tragopogon pratensis*	yellow goat's beard	0		alien	0
graminoid	Poaceae	*Tridens flavus*	grease grass	1		native	1
forb/herb	Fabaceae	*Trifolium hybridum*	alsike clover	0		alien	0
forb/herb	Fabaceae	*Trifolium pratense*	red clover	0		alien	0
forb/herb	Fabaceae	*Trifolium repens*	white clover	0		alien	0
forb/herb	Campanulaceae	*Triodanis perfoliata*	venus'- looking-glass	2		native	1
forb/herb	Caprifoliaceae	*Triosteum angustifolium*	lesser horse-gentian	5		native	1

Type	Family	Scientific Name	Common Name	Ohio COC[1]	Ohio Prairie Indicator[2]	Class[3]	Source[4]
forb/herb	Brassicaceae	*Turritis glabra*	tower mustard	3	X	native	1
tree	Ulmaceae	*Ulmus americana*	American elm	2		native	1
tree	Ulmaceae	*Ulmus pumila*	Siberian elm	0		alien	0
tree	Ulmaceae	*Ulmus rubra*	slippery elm	3		native	1
tree	Urticaceae	*Urtica dioica var. procera*	Tall nettle	1		native	1
forb/herb	Valerianaceae	*Valerianella umbilicata*	beaked corn salad	2		native	1
forb/herb	Scrophulariaceae	*Verbascum blattaria*	moth mullein	0		alien	0
forb/herb	Scrophulariaceae	*Verbascum phoeniceum*	purple mullein	0		alien	0
forb/herb	Scrophulariaceae	*Verbascum thaspus*	common mullein	0		alien	0
forb/herb	Verbenaceae	*Verbena hastata*	blue vervain	4	X	native	2
forb/herb	Verbenaceae	*Verbena stricta*	hoary vervain	3	X	native	1
forb/herb	Verbenaceae	*Verbena urticifolia*	white vervain	3		native	1
forb/herb	Asteraceae	*Verbesina alternifolia*	wingstem	5		native	1
forb/herb	Asteraceae	*Verbesina helianthoides*	hairy wingstem	5	X	native	2
forb/herb	Asteraceae	*Vernonia gigantea*	tall ironweed	2		native	1
forb/herb	Asteraceae	*Veronia arvensis*	corn speedwell	0		alien	0
forb/herb	Scrophulariaceae	*Veronicastrum virginicum*	Culver's-root	7	X	native	2
forb/herb	Violaceae	*Viola bicolor*	American field pansy	2		native	4
forb/herb	Violaceae	*Viola sororia*	common blue violet	1	X	native	1
forb/herb	Violaceae	*Viola striata*	striped creamy violet	5		native	1
vine	Vitaceae	*Vitis cinerea*	pigeon grape	6		native	4
vine	Vitaceae	*Vitis riparia*	riverbank grape	3		native	1

Notes

Introduction

1. Arthur George Renstrom, *Wilbur and Orville Wright—A Reissue of a Chronology Commemorating the Hundredth Anniversary of the Birth of Orville Wright, August 19, 1871* (Washington, D.C.: National Aeronautics and Space Administration, Office of External Relations, 2003), 84.

1. A Grid on the Land

1. W. H. Hunter, comp., "Pathfinders of Jefferson County," *Ohio Archaeological and Historical Publications* 6 (1900): 170.

2. Ohio History Connection, Public land survey system notes for Township 3, Range 8, and Township 2, Range 8, Between the Miamis Survey, Ohio History Center, Library/Archives/Library Research Room, microfiche reels GR8424 and GR8425.

3. C. Albert White, *A History of the Rectangular Survey System* (Washington, D.C.: U.S. Department of the Interior, Bureau of Land Management, 1983), 11–13.

4. Robert B. Gordon, *The Natural Vegetation of Ohio in Pioneer Days* (Columbus: Ohio State Univ. Press, 1969), 15–19.

5. H. B. Teetor, *Life and Times of Israel Ludlow* (Cincinnati: Cranston & Stowe, 1885), 7.

6. Lewis H. Garrard, *Memoir of Charlotte Chambers* (Philadelphia: T. K. & P. G. Collins, 1868), 18.

7. George W. Knepper, *The Ohio Lands Book* (Columbus: Ohio Auditor of State, 2002), 31.

8. Bill Pickard, "Israel Ludlow: The Man That Surveyed Ohio," *Archaeology Blog*, Nov. 10, 2009, https://www.ohiohistory.org/learn/collections/archaeology/archaeology-blog/2009/november-2009/israel-ludlow-the-man-that-surveyed-ohio.

9. Garrard, *Memoir of Charlotte Chambers,* 23–25.

10. Robert W. Steele and Mary Davies Steel, *Early Dayton* (Dayton: W. B. Publishing House, W. J. Shuey Publisher, 1896), 216.

11. Garrard, *Memoir of Charlotte Chambers,* 31, 28, 34.

12. Ibid., 48–49.

13. James L. Williams, *Blazes, Posts, and Stones, A History of Ohio's Original Land Subdivisions.* (Akron: University of Akron Press, 2015), 375.

14. Garrard, *Memoir of Charlotte Chambers,* 53.

2. Ice, Water, and Fire

1. Stanley E. Norris, William P. Cross, and Richard P. Goldthwait, *The Water Resources of Greene County, Ohio,* Bulletin no. 19 (Columbus: Ohio Department of Natural Resources, Division of Water, 1956), 4.

2. Alfred D. Dachnowski, *Peat Deposits of Ohio, Ohio Geological Survey Bulletin* 16 (1912): 67–69; Denise H. Dumouchelle and Jeffrey T. de Roche, *Lithologic, Natural-Gamma, Grain Size, and Well-Construction Data for Wright-Patterson Air Force Base, Ohio,* Open-File Report 91–181 (Washington, D.C.: U.S. Geological Survey, 1991), 38–39.

3. William C. Walton and George D. Scudder, *Ground Water Resources of the Valley Train Deposits in the Fairborn Area, Technical Report #3* (Columbus: Ohio Division of Natural Resources, Division of Water, 1960), 12.

4. Gregory A. Schumacher et al., "Geology of the Dayton Region in Core and Outcrop: A Workshop and Field Trip for Citizens, Environmental Investigators, Geologists, and Educators," Ohio Department of Natural Resources, Division of Geological Survey Open-File Report, 2012, 3, available online at the Ohio Department of Natural Resources Web site, https://geosurvey.ohiodnr .gov/portals/geosurvey/PDFs/OpenFileReports/OFR_2012–1.pdf.

5. Ibid.

6. Michael C. Hansen, comp., "The Teays River," *Ohio Department of Natural Resources, Division of Geological Survey GeoFacts, No. 10,* Nov. 1995, https:// geosurvey.ohiodnr.gov/portals/geosurvey/PDFs/GeoFacts/geof10.pdf.

7. Norris, Cross, and Goldthwait, "Water Resources of Greene County, Ohio," 12.

8. Hansen, "Teays River," 1.

9. Schumacher et al., "Geology of the Dayton Region in Core and Outcrop," 3.

10. Michael C. Hansen, "The Ice Age in Ohio," *Ohio Department of Natural Resources Division of Geological Survey,* 2008, https://geosurvey.ohiodnr.gov/ portals/geosurvey/PDFs/Education/el07.pdf.

11. Richard P. Goldthwait, "Scenes in Ohio during the Last Ice Age," address of the president of the Ohio Academy of Science delivered at the Sixty-Eighth Annual Meeting at Capital University, Bexley, Ohio, April 17, 1959, reprinted in the *Ohio Journal of Science* 111, nos. 2–5 (2013): 7.

12. Benjamin H. Richard et al., *Delineation of the Ancestral Drainage Paths of the Mad River, Near Dayton, Ohio,* Wright State University Department of Geology technical report series, report GP 7904 RK, 1979.

13. Schumacher et al., *Geology of the Dayton Region in Core and Outcrop,* 3, 18.

14. Dumouchelle and de Roche, *Lithologic, Natural-Gamma, Grain Size, and Well-Construction Data,* 4.

15. James P. Amon et al., "Temperate Zone Fens of the Glaciated Midwestern USA," *Wetlands* 22, no. 2 (2002): 313.

16. Michael A. Kost et al., *Natural Communities of Michigan: Classification and Description, Michigan Natural Features Inventory,* Report Number 2007–21 (Lansing: Michigan Department of Natural Resources Wildlife Division and Forest, Mineral and Fire Management Division, 2007.)

17. Ronald L. Stuckey and Guy L. Denny, "Prairie Fens and Bog Fens in Ohio: Floristic Similarities, Differences, and Geographic Affinities," in *Geobotany II,* ed. R. C. Romans (New York: Plenum, 1981), 4.

18. Michael B. Lafferty, *Ohio's Natural Heritage* (Columbus: Ohio Academy of Science, 1979), 38.

19. Stuckey and Denny, "Prairie Fens and Bog Fens in Ohio," 6.

20. Lafferty, *Ohio's Natural Heritage,* 134, 136.

21. Stuckey and Denny, "Prairie Fens and Bog Fens in Ohio," 6.

22. Clara May Frederick, "A Natural History Study of the Vascular Flora of Cedar Bog, Champaign County, Ohio," *Ohio Journal of Science* 74 (Mar. 1974): 65.

23. Alan J. Woods et al., *Ecoregions of Indiana and Ohio* (Reston, VA: U.S. Dept. of the Interior, U.S. Geological Survey, 1998).

24. David Nolin, unpublished map of prairies and fens of the Mad River Valley, compiled from surveyor records, 2016.

25. Heather Pringle, "The First Americans," *Scientific American,* Nov. 2011, 40; Bradley T. Lepper, *Ohio Archaeology, An Illustrated Chronicle of Ancient American Indian Cultures* (Wilmington, OH: Orange Frazer Press, 2005) 26.

26. Ibid., ix.

27. Jennifer R. Haas, Michael F. Kolb, and John D. Richards, *Archaeology, Geomorphology, and Land Use History at Wright-Patterson Air Force Base, Ohio* (Milwaukee: Great Lakes Archaeological Research Center, 1996), 103.

28. Jerry E. Clark, *The Shawnee* (Lexington: Univ. Press of Kentucky, 1993), 7, 24.

29. R. S. Dills, *History of Greene County Together with Historic Notes on the Northwest and the State of Ohio* (Dayton: Odell & Mayer, 1881) 710.

30. Omer C. Stewart; *Forgotten Fires: Native Americans and the Transient Wilderness,* ed. Henry T. Anderson and Kat Lewis (Norman: Univ. of Oklahoma Press, 2002), 70–312.

31. Stephen R. Jones and Ruth Carol Cushman, *The North American Prairie: A Field Guide to the Plants, Wildlife, and Natural History of the Prairie Including Where to Hike and Camp* (Boston: Houghton Mifflin, 2004), 17.

32. Stewart, *Forgotten Fires: Native Americans and the Transient Wilderness,* 115, 78, 76.

33. Ibid., 77–78.

34. William M. Darlington, *An Account of the Remarkable Occurrences in the Life and Travels of Col. James Smith during His Captivity with the Indians, in the Years 1755, '56. '57, '58, and '59* (Cincinnati: Robert Clarke Co., 1907), 86–88.

35. Dills, *History of Greene County,* 720.

3. Early Exploration and Settlement

1. William M. Darlington, *Christopher Gist's Journals with Historical, Geographical, and Ethnological Notes, and Biographies of His Contemporaries* (Cincinnati: Robert Clarke Co., 1907), 31, 47, 56.

2. Augustus Waldo Drury, *History of the City of Dayton and Montgomery County, Ohio,* 2 vols. (Dayton: S. J. Clarke, 1909), 1:93.

3. Robert W. Steele and Mary Davies Steele, *Early Dayton* (Dayton: U. B. Publishing House, W. J. Shuey Publisher, 1896), 20, 21.

4. Drury, *History of the City of Dayton,* 66–67, 21.

5. Steele and Steele, *Early Dayton,* 22.

6. Drury, *History of the City of Dayton,* 69.

7. Ibid., 93.

8. Louis L. Chmiel, *Ohio: Home of the Wright Brothers, Birthplace of Aviation: The Genealogical Chronicle of an Ohio Pioneer Family and the Invention of the Airplane 1776–1948,* ed. Ann Vallo Febus (Dayton: Louis L. Chmiel, 2013), 27, 62.

9. John F. Edgar, *Pioneer Life in Dayton and Vicinity, 1796–1840* (Dayton: U.B. Publishing House, W. J. Shuey Publisher, 1896), 23.

10. R. S. Dills, *History of Greene County Together with Historic Notes on the Northwest and the State of Ohio* (Dayton: Odell & Mayer, 1881), 710.

11. Drury, *History of the City of Dayton,* 88.

12. Ibid., 88–89.

13. James L. Williams, *Blazes, Posts, and Stones, A History of Ohio's Original Land Subdivisions* (Akron: Univ. of Akron Press, 2015), 362.

14. Charlotte Reeve Conover, *Dayton, Ohio: An Intimate History* (New York: Lewis Historical Publishing, 1932), 19.

15. Beverly W. Bond Jr., ed., "Memoirs of Benjamin Van Cleve," *Quarterly Publication of the Historical and Philosophical Society of Ohio* 17 (Jan.–June 1922): 57.

16. George W. Knepper, *The Ohio Lands Book* (Columbus: Ohio Auditor of State, 2002), 36–38.

17. U.S. Department of the Interior, Bureau of Land Management, *General Land Office Records,* accessed Feb. 17, 2016, http://www.glorecords.blm.gov.

18. Michael B. Lafferty, *Ohio's Natural Heritage* (Columbus: Ohio Academy of Science, 1979), 296.

19. John Leonard Riddell, "Synopsis of the Flora of the Western States," *Western Journal of the Medical and Physical Sciences* 8 (1834): 497, republished in 1835 by E. Deming in Cincinnati as a stand-alone volume.

20. Ronald L. Stuckey and James S. Pringle, "Type Localities of Vascular Plants First Described from Ohio," *SIDA Contributions to Botany* 20, no. 4 (2003): 1687.

21. Riddell, "Synopsis of the Flora of the Western States," 497.

22. John Van Cleve, map of farm, notebook 4: Miscellaneous Notes, Undated, Van Cleve–Dover Collection, Dayton Metro Library, Dayton.

23. Steele and Steele, *Early Dayton,* 67.

24. Benjamin Van Cleve to John Van Cleve, July 17, 1818, folder 1, box 6, Van Cleve–Dover Collection.

25. John Van Cleve, map of Dayton, 1839, item 5, folder 1, drawer 1, cabinet 2, Map Collection, Van Cleve–Dover Collection.

26. Steele and Steele, *Early Dayton,* 69.

27. Agnes Anderson Hall, "Letters from John," unpublished manuscript, S.1: S.n, [n.d.]. [Dayton B V2224H], 89, 105, 261, Dayton Metro Library, Dayton.

28. Ibid., 107.

29. Larry Morse, "John W. Van Cleve, Pioneer Ohio Botanist," 3, summary of presentation to the Ohio Academy of Science, April 21, 1967, copy in possession of David Nolin.

30. John W. Van Cleve's copy of John Torrey, *A Compendium of the Flora of the Northern and Middle States: Containing Generic and Specific Descriptions of All the Plants, Exclusive of the Cryptogamia, Hitherto Found in the United States North of the Potomac* (New York: S. B. Collins, 1826), in Van Cleve–Dover Collection.

31. John W. Van Cleve to John Torrey, Aug. 27, 1838, folder 11, box 3, Van Cleve–Dover Collection.

32. Morse, "John W. Van Cleve."

33. Hall, "Letters from John," 195–96.

34. Untitled poem, folder 1, box 4, subser. 5, ser. 2, Van Cleve–Dover Collection.

35. Ohio History Connection, "Turnpikes, in *Ohio History Central,* accessed Feb. 17, 2016, http://www.ohiohistorycentral.org/w/Turnpikes.

36. Steele and Steele, *Early Dayton,* 235, 168–69.

37. Forty-Third General Assembly of the State of Ohio, *Acts of a General Nature Passed by the Forty-third General Assembly of the State of Ohio* (Columbus: Samuel Medary, State Printer, 1845), 302–4.

38. Steele and Steele, *Early Dayton,* 236.

39. William P. Huffman, transcript of presentation on the history of the Huffman family made on September 1, 1962, 2. This manuscript was in the files of Mr. Tony Huffman, a resident of Dayton and descendent of the first William Huffman who moved to Dayton.

40. Steele and Steele, *Early Dayton,* 111.

41. U.S. Department of the Interior, *General Land Office Records.*

42. Huffman, transcript, 3.

43. Harvey W. Crew, *History of Dayton, Ohio* (Dayton: United Brethren Publishing, 1889), 696.

44. U.S. Census Bureau, Schedule 4, *Production of Agriculture in Bath Township in the County of Greene in the Post Office Osborn,* 1860, 29.

45. Crew, *History of Dayton,* 696.

46. Levi Riddell and W. D. Riddell, *Riddell's Atlas of Greene County* (Xenia, OH: Levi and W. D. Riddell, 1896), 17.

47. William C. Walton and George D. Scudder*, Ground Water Resources of the Valley Train Deposits in the Fairborn Area, Technical Report #3* (Columbus: Ohio Division of Natural Resources, Division of Water, 1960), 37–38.

48. Ohio History Connection, Original Surveyors Records for Township 3, Range 8, and Township 2, Range 8, Between the Miamis Survey, microfiche reels GR8424 and GR8425, Ohio History Center Library/Archives/Library Research Room.

49. Dills, *History of Greene County,* 719.

50. George F. Robinson, *History of Greene County, Ohio: Embracing the Organization of the County . . .* (Xenia, OH: S. J. Clarke, 1902, 52).

51. Probate of Joseph Smith, Will Record, Greene County Probate Court, Ancestry.com; *Ohio, Wills and Probate Records, 1786–1998* [database on-line] (Provo, UT: Ancestry.com, 2015), original data: Ohio County, District and Probate Courts, 242–43.

52. Deed transferring the Fairfield Mill and Race from Jacob Smith to Robert C. Crawford, Deed records, vol. 13, 101–3, Greene County Archives, Xenia, OH.

53. Property taxes paid by Robert Crawford, tax records for Bath Township, books 1835–44, Greene County Archives.

54. D. W. Garber, *Waterwheels and Millstones: A History of Ohio Gristmills and Milling* (Columbus: Ohio Historical Society, 1970), 72.

55. Frick Ditch, Greene County Commission Ditch Records, vol. 1, 7–107, Greene County Archives.

56. Meeting Record of the Bath Township Trustees, Dec. 15, 1848–Apr. 12, 1869, Fairfield (Greene County), book 2, 101, 94, 194–95, Archives of Bath Township, Greene County Archives.

57. Frick Ditch, 89–90.

58. Frick Ditch Alteration, Greene County Commission Ditch Records, vol. 2, 1865, 1–11, Greene County Archives.

59. J. R. Swan, *Revised Statutes of the State of Ohio, of a General Nature* (Cincinnati: R. Clarke & Co., 1870), 523–28.

60. John H. Klippart, *The Principles and Practice of Land Drainage: A Brief History of Underdraining* . . . (Cincinnati: Robert Clarke & Co., 1861), 27, 31–32.

61. Ibid., 173–76, 183.

62. Zachary Sugg, "Assessing U.S. Farm Drainage: Can GIS Lead to Better Estimates of Subsurface Drainage Extent?" World Resources Institute, 2007, available online at http://pdf.wri.org/assessing_farm_drainage.pdf, 6.

4. The World's First Airfield

1. Tom Crouch, *The Bishop's Boys: A Life of Wilbur and Orville Wright* (New York: Norton, 1989), 268.

2. Ibid., 279.

3. Roz Young, "Bicycle Enthusiasm Sparked Friendship with the Wrights," *Dayton Daily News,* Sept. 6, 1997; Tom Crouch, *Bishop's Boys,* 279.

4. Marla McEnaney et al., *From Pasture to Runway: Huffman Prairie Flying Field, Wright-Patterson Air Force Base, Cultural Landscape Report, Landscape Implementation Plan, Interpretation Plan* (Washington, D.C.: U.S. Department of the Interior, 2002), 9.

5. Crouch, *Bishop's Boys,* 278–79.

6. Ibid., 283, 284.

7. Arthur George Renstrom, *Wilbur and Orville Wright: A Reissue of a Chronology Commemorating the Hundredth Anniversary of the Birth of Orville Wright, August 19, 1871* (Washington, D.C.: National Aeronautics and Space Administration, Office of External Relations, 2003), 84.

8. Crouch, *Bishop's Boys,* 172–73.

9. Young, "Bicycle Enthusiasm Sparked Friendship with the Wrights."

10. Lois E. Walker and Shelby E. Wickam, *From Huffman Prairie to the Moon: The History of Wright-Patterson Air Force Base* ([Dayton]: WPAFB, Office of History, 2750th Air Base Wing, 1986), 14.

11. Edward J. Roach, *The Wright Company: From Invention to Industry* (Athens: Ohio University Press, 2013), 2.

5. From Floodplain to Air Force Base

1. Arthur E. Morgan, *The Miami Conservancy District,* (New York: McGraw-Hill, 1951), 12, 24, 47; Carl M. Becker and Patrick B. Nolan, *Keeping the Promise* (Dayton: Landfall Press, 1988), 43, 47.

2. Miami Conservancy District, "Paying for the Flood Prevention Project," *Miami Conservancy District Bulletin* 3, nos. 11 and 12 (1951): 256–57, 168–71.

3. Morgan, *Miami Conservancy District,* 255, 257.

4. Ibid., 419.

5. Ibid., 346–48.

6. Department of the Air Force, *Home Field Advantage: A Century of Partnership between Wright-Patterson Air Force Base and Dayton, Ohio, in the Pursuit of Aeronautical Excellence* (Washington, D.C.: U.S. Superintendent of Documents, 2004), 51.

7. Ibid., 55.

8. "Annual Report, Signal Corps, Aviation School, Wilbur Wright Field, Fairfield, Ohio, May 31, 1918, signed by Maj. Arthur E. Wilbourn, Commanding Officer," 1–2, Wright-Patterson Air Force Base Archives.

9. "Wilbur Wright Field Chosen for Aviation," *Dayton Daily News,* Sept. 15, 1918.

10. Graham Smith to Ezra M. Kuhns, Nov. 27, 1922, Miami Conservancy District Records, MS-128, file 3, 1–2, box 17, ser. IF, Wright State University Archives and Special Collections, Dayton.

11. A. M. Jacobs, "Will She Fly?" *Popular Mechanics,* Mar. 1929, 379–85.

12. Walker and Wickam, *From Huffman Prairie to the Moon: The History of Wright-Patterson Air Force Base* ([Dayton]:WPAFB: Office of History, 2750th Air Base Wing, 1986), 111.

13. Smith to Kuhns, Nov. 27, 1922.

14. Morgan, *Miami Conservancy District,* 346–48.

15. Walker and Wickam, *From Huffman Prairie to the Moon,* 112.

16. Department of the Air Force, *Home Field Advantage,* 99, 98.

17. Michael Gough, *The Pulitzer Air Races, American Aviation and Speed Supremacy, 1920–1925* (Jefferson, NC: McFarland, 2013), 158–59.

18. Peter Vischer, "When Men Race with Death to Make the Air Safe," *Popular Science Monthly,* Jan. 1925, 36.

19. Walker and Wickam, *From Huffman Prairie to the Moon,* 64.

20. James J. Cooke, *Billy Mitchell* (Boulder, CO: Lynne Rienner, 2002), 54.

21. Harold S. Sharp, *The Courtmartial of Billy Mitchell (1925)* (Metuchen, NJ: Scarecrow, 1977), 430–33.

22. Walker and Wickam, *From Huffman Prairie to the Moon,* 257.

23. Ibid., 270–71.

24. Ibid., 290.

25. Department of the Air Force, *Home Field Advantage,* 192–93.

26. Nationwide Environmental Tile Research, "Wright-Patterson Air Force Base Superfund National Priorities List (NPL) Site," NETR Online, Oct. 4, 1989, http://environment.netronline.com/site.php?cid=OH7571724312.

27. National Environmental Tile Research, "Wright-Patterson Air Force Base Superfund National Priorities List (NPL) Site," and NPL Fact Sheet, Jan. 2004, both at EPA Superfund Site, Wright Patterson Air Force Base, Dayton, Ohio, https://cumulis.epa.gov/supercpad/cursites/dsp_ssppSiteData1.cfm?id=050
4939, https://cumulis.epa.gov/supercpad/cursites/csitinfo.cfm?id=0504939.

28. Marla McEnaney et al., *From Pasture to Runway, Huffman Prairie Flying Field, Wright-Patterson Air Force Base, Cultural Landscape Report, Landscape Implementation Plan, Interpretation Plan* (Washington, D.C.: U.S. Department of the Interior, 2002), 52, available online at the National Park Service Web site, https://www.nps.gov/daav/getinvolved/upload/HPFF-CLR.pdf.

29. Wright-Patterson Air Force Base, *Integrated Natural Resources Management Plan,* 71.

30. McEnaney et al., *From Pasture to Runway,* 52.

31. Agnes Anderson Hall, "Letters from John," unpublished manuscript in Dayton Metro Library, S.1: S.n, [n.d.]. [Dayton B V2224H], 254

6. A Prairie Renaissance

1. Michael B. Lafferty, *Ohio's Natural Heritage* (Columbus: Ohio Academy of Science, 1979), 134; David B. Nolin and James R. Runkle, "Prairies and Fens of Bath Township, Greene County, Ohio: 1802 and 1984," *Ohio Journal of Science* 85, no. 3 (1985): 125.

2. Robert Moeller, "Methods of Development Used at the Aullwood Audubon Center, Dayton, Ohio," *Ohio Journal of Science* 73, no. 5 (1973): 307.

3. Allison W. Cusick and K. Roger Troutman, *The Prairie Survey Project: A Summary of Data to Date.* Ohio Biological Survey Informative Circular No. 10 (Columbus: Ohio State Univ., 1978), 1.

4. John Blakeman, president, Ohio Prairie Association, interview with David Nolin, Jan. 21, 2016.

5. Nolin and Runkle, "Prairies and Fens of Bath Township," 129.

6. Paul Knoop, "Nature Comes to Base on a Wing and a Prairie," *Dayton Daily News,* July 25, 1985.

7. Guy L. Denny to Terri Lucas, Dec. 17, 1984, personal collection of David Nolin.

8. Ohio Department of Natural Resources, *Division of Natural Areas and Preserves Newsletter* 8, no. 3 (June 1986): 1.

9. Cusick and Troutman, "Prairie Survey Project," iv.

10. Jim McCormac and Gary Meszaros, *Wild Ohio: The Best of Our Natural Heritage* (Kent, OH: Kent State University Press, 2009), 45–47.

11. Ohio Department of Natural Resources, "Milford Center Prairie State Natural Area," Division of Natural Areas and Preserves, accessed May 27, 2016, http://naturepreserves.ohiodnr.gov/state-nature-preserves/find-a-state-nature-preserve/milford-center-prairie; Ohio Prairie Association, "Claridon Prairie,"

Ohio Prairie Association Web site, accessed June 21, 2017, http://www.ohio -prairie.org/page83.html.

12. John E. Weaver, *Prairie Plants and Their Environment* (Lincoln: Univ. of Nebraska Press, 1968), 195–207.

13. Miami Conservancy District, *1915 Topographic Survey Map of Huffman Reservoir Site,* Dwg #1761, sheet 3, copy in possession of David Nolin.

14. "Cooperative Agreement between the Department of Defense (DoD) and The Nature Conservancy (TNC)," signed December 13, 1988, available online at the U.S. Army Corps of Engineers Web site, http://www.usace.army .mil/Portals/2/docs/civilworks/mous/tnc_mou.pdf.

15. David Minney, "Management and Breeding Birds on a Tallgrass Prairie Remnant, 1990–1993; Huffman Prairie, Ohio," internal document (Columbus: Ohio Chapter of The Nature Conservancy, 1993), 5.

16. Eric H. Metzler and Roger A. Zebold, "Huffman Prairie Inventory of Lepidoptera, June through December 1992, Prepared for The Nature Conservancy, Ohio Chapter, and Wright-Patterson Air Force Base, 31 December, 1992," 13, copy can be obtained from WPAFB Natural Resources Program, 88th Air Base Wing Environmental Branch.

17. Eric H. Metzler and Roger A. Zebold, "Brief Note: Twenty-eight Species of Moths New to Ohio from Huffman Prairie, Greene County," *Ohio Journal of Science* 95 (June 1995): 240–42.

18. David Minney, "Huffman Prairie Baseline Data, Submitted to Wright-Patterson Air Force Base" (Columbus: Ohio Chapter of The Nature Conservancy. 1990), 1, copy can be obtained from WPAFB Natural Resources Program, 88th Air Base Wing Environmental Branch.

19. Scott J. Meiners and David L. Gorchov, "The Soil Seed Pool of Huffman Prairie, a Degraded Ohio Prairie, and Its Potential in Restoration," *Ohio Journal of Science* 94, no. 4 (1994): 85.

20. Ohio Chapter of The Nature Conservancy, "Huffman Prairie Management Plan, Prepared for Wright-Patterson Air Force Base by The Nature Conservancy, Ohio Chapter, March 23, 1994" (Columbus: Ohio Chapter of The Nature Conservancy, 1994), 2–3, in possession of David Nolin.

21. Ohio Chapter of The Nature Conservancy, "Ron and Liz Cramer Receive Award," *Volunteers! Newsletter,* Spring 1995.

22. Jennifer A. Hillmer, Nomination form for the President's Stewardship Award, submitted to The Nature Conservancy Home Office, Sept. 19, 1996, copy in possession of David Nolin.

23. Amec Earth and Environmental, Inc., Huffman Prairie Assessment and Workplan, prepared for Wright-Patterson Air Force Base, 15, submitted to Wright-Patterson Air Force Base, 2007, copy can be obtained from WPAFB Natural Resources Program, 88th Air Base Wing Environmental Branch.

24. Ohio Invasive Plants Council, "Smooth Brome," *Invasive Plants of Ohio, Fact Sheet 13,* accessed May 27, 2016, http://www.oipc.info/uploads/5/8/6/ 5/58652481/13factsheetsmoothbrome.pdf.

25. David Minney, "Huffman Prairie: Plant Community Monitoring Report, 2014," 12, submitted to Five Rivers MetroParks, copy can be obtained from WPAFB Natural Resources Program, 88th Air Base Wing Environmental Branch.

26. Wright-Patterson Air Force Base, Environmental Assessment to Implement the Integrated Natural Resources Management Plan, Wright-Patterson

Air Force Base, Ohio, 88th Civil Engineer Group, Sept. 2016, http://www.wpafb
.af.mil/Portals/60/documents/Index/environmental/160913-Environmental
-Natural-resources-management-plan.pdf?ver=2016–09–13–140613–413.

27. Beaver Creek Wetlands Association, "Siebenthaler Fen," Beaver Creek
Wetlands Association, 2012, http://www.beavercreekwetlands.org/maplocations
-siebenthaler.html; Clark County Park District, "Leadingham Prairie and Nature
Preserve," Clark County Park District, accessed June 11, 2017. http://www.clark
countyparks.org/our-parks-trails/leadingham-prairie/.

28. Gene Barnett, "Ohio EPA Awards Grant for Huffman Prairie," Wright-
Patterson Air Force Base Web site, January 23, 2015. http://www.wpafb.af.mil
/News/Article-Display/Article/818860/ohio-epa-awards-grant-for-huffman
-prairie.

7. Plants and Animals of Huffman Prairie State Natural Landmark

1. "Huffman Prairie Flying Field," *eBird: An Online Database of Bird Distribution and Abundance,* accessed: June 10, 2017, http://ebird.org/ebird/
hotspot/L2132447?yr=all&m=&rank=mrec.

2. James S. McCormac and Gregory Kennedy, *Birds of Ohio* (Auburn, WA:
Lone Pine, 2004), 310.

3. Paul G. Rodewald et al., eds., *The Second Atlas of Breeding Birds in Ohio*
(University Park: Pennsylvania State Univ. Press, 2016), 412–17.

4. Peter Schramm, David S. Schramm, and Stephen G. Johnson, "Seasonal
Phenology and Habitat Selection of the Sedge Wren *Cistothorus plantensis* in
a Restored Tallgrass Prairie," in *The Prairie: Past, Present, and Future: Proceedings of the Ninth North American Prairie Conference, Held July 29–August 1,
1984, Moorhead, Minnesota,* ed. Gary K. Clambey and Richard H. Pemble
(Fargo: Tri-College Univ. Center for Environmental Studies, North Dakota
State Univ., 1986), 95–98.

5. Benedict J. Blinco, *The Birds of Dayton and the Central Miami Valley,*
Ohio Biological Survey, Biological Notes, no. 1 (Columbus: Ohio State Univ.
1964), 53.

6. John Nolan, "C-5 Cargo Planes to Be Replaced by C-17s," *Dayton Daily
News,* Mar. 12, 2010.

7. Brian E. Washburn and Thomas W. Seamans, "Managing Turfgrass to
Reduce Wildlife Hazards at Airports," and James A. Martin et al., "Wildlife
Conservation and Alternative Land Uses at Airports," both in *Wildlife in Air-
port Environments: Preventing Animal-Aircraft Collisions Through Science-Based
Management,* ed. Travis L. DeVault, Bradley F. Blackwell, and Jerrold L. Belant
(Baltimore: Johns Hopkins Univ. Press, 2013), 122–23, 106.

8. U.S. Fish and Wildlife, "Indiana Bat (*Myotis sodalis*)," *Endangered Species,* last updated July 19, 2016, http://www.fws.gov/midwest/endangered/
mammals/inba/inbafctsht.html.

9. BHE Environmental Management, *A Mist Net Survey and Telemetry Study
of Indiana Bats at Wright-Patterson Air Force Base in Greene and Montgomery
Counties, Ohio,* 33, 27. This report may be obtained from the WPAFB Natural
Resources Program, 88th Air Base Wing Environmental Branch.

10. Ohio Department of Natural Resources, "Massasauga—*Sistrurus catenatus catenatus,*" *ODNR Division of Wildlife/Species and Habitats/Species*

Guide Index/Reptiles, accessed April 26, 2017, http://wildlife.ohiodnr.gov/species-and-habitats/species-guide-index/reptiles/massasauga; U.S. Fish and Wildlife Service, Eastern Massasauga (*Sistrurus catenatus*) Status: Proposed at Threatened," *U.S. Fish and Wildlife Service Endangered Species,* accessed June 10, 2017, http://www.fws.gov/midwest/endangered/reptiles/eama/.

11. "Reaches for Cucumber—Uncovers Rattlesnake," *Skywrighter,* Aug. 26, 1960.

12. Florence Brown, "Rare Massasaugas Make Home on Base," *Skywrighter,* July 16, 1993.

13. Jeffrey G. Davis, "Eastern Massasauga at Wright-Patterson Air Force Base in Dayton, Ohio," submitted to WPAFB, 2015, 8. This report may be obtained from the WPAFB Natural Resources Program, 88th Air Base Wing Environmental Branch.

14. Ohio Department of Natural Resources Division of Wildlife, "Smooth Greensnake—Opheodrys vernalis," *ODNR Division of Wildlife/Species and Habitats/Species Guide Index/Reptiles,* accessed June 10, 2017, http://wildlife.ohiodnr.gov/species-and-habitats/species-guide-index/reptiles/smooth-greensnake.

15. Davis, "Eastern Massasauga at Wright-Patterson Air Force Base," 13.

16. Eric H. Metzler and Roger A. Zebold, "Brief Note: Twenty-eight Species of Moths New to Ohio from Huffman Prairie, Greene County," *Ohio Journal of Science* 95 (June 1995): 240–42.

17. Eric H. Metzler and David Adamski, "A New Species of Gnorimoschema Busck, 1900 (*Lepidoptera: Gelechiidae, Gelechiinae*) from Ohio and Illinois," *Fabreries* 27, no. 1 (2002): 59–68; David Adamski and Eric H. Metzler, "A New Species of Glyphidocera Walsingham from Southwestern Ohio (*Lepidoptera: Gelechioidea: Glyphidoceridae*)," *Proceedings of the Entomologial Society of Washington* 102, no. 2 (2000): 301.

18. Ohio Department of Natural Resources Division of Wildlife. "Bees and Wasps of Ohio," Publication 5488 (0316) (Columbus: Ohio Division of Wildlife, 2016), 20.

19. Steve Bennish, "Effort to Increase Bee Population Launched in Dayton," *Dayton Daily News,* June 22, 2015.

Bibliography

Archives

Dayton Metro Library, Dayton, Ohio.
Greene County Archives, Xenia, Ohio.
Ohio History Connection. Ohio History Center Library/Archives/Library Research Room. Columbus.
Wright-Patterson Air Force Base Archives.
Wright State University Archives and Special Collections, Dayton, Ohio.

Published Sources

Adamski, David, and Eric H. Metzler. "A New Species of Glyphodocera Walsingham from Southwestern Ohio (*Lepidoptera: Gelechioidea: Glyphidoceridae*)." *Proceedings of the Entomologial Society of Washington* 102, no. 2 (2000): 301–7.

Amec Earth and Environmental. "Huffman Prairie Assessment and Workplan, prepared for Wright-Patterson Air Force Base." Submitted to Wright-Patterson Air Force Base, Natural Resources Program, 88th Air Base Wing Environmental Branch, 2007. Copy can be obtained from WPAFB Natural Resources Program, 88th Air Base Wing Environmental Branch.

Amon, James P, Carol A. Thompson, Quentin Carpenter, and James Miner. "Temperate Zone Fens of the Glaciated Midwestern USA," *Wetlands* 22, no. 2 (2002): 313.

Barnett, Gene. "Ohio EPA Awards Grant for Huffman Prairie." Wright-Patterson Air Force Base Web site, January 23, 2015, http://www.wpafb.af.mil/News/Article-Display/Article/818860/ohio-epa-awards-grant-for-huffman-prairie.

Beaver Creek Wetlands Association. "Siebenthaler Fen." *Beaver Creek Wetlands Association.* 2012. http://www.beavercreekwetlands.org/maplocations-siebenthaler.html

Becker, Carl M., and Patrick B. Nolan, *Keeping the Promise.* Dayton: Landfall Press, 1988.

Bennish, Steve. "Effort to Increase Bee Population Launched in Dayton." *Dayton Daily News,* June 22, 2015.

BHE Environmental Management. "A Mist Net Survey and Telemetry Study of Indiana Bats at Wright-Patterson Air Force Base in Greene and Montgomery Counties, Ohio." Prepared for Wright-Patterson Air Force Base 88th Air Base Wing, Office of Environmental Management, Cincinnati: BHE Environmental Management, 2001. Copy can be obtained from WPAFB Natural Resources Program, 88th Air Base Wing, Environmental Branch.

Blincoe, Benjamin J. *The Birds of Dayton and the Central Miami Valley.* Ohio Biological Survey, Biological Notes, no. 1. Columbus: Ohio State University, 1964.

Bond, Beverly, Jr., ed. "Memoirs of Benjamin Van Cleve." *Quarterly Publication of the Historical and Philosophical Society of Ohio* 17 (January–June 1922): 3–71.

Brown, Florence. "Rare Massasaugas Make Home on Base." *Skywrighter,* July 16, 1993.

Chmiel, Louis L. *Ohio: Home of the Wright Brothers: Birthplace of Aviation: The Genealogical Chronicle of an Ohio Pioneer Family and the Invention of the Airplane 1776–1948.* Edited by Ann Vallo Febus. Dayton: Louis L. Chmiel, 2013.

Clark, Jerry E. *The Shawnee.* Lexington: University Press of Kentucky, 1993.

Clark County Park District. "Leadingham Prairie Preserve." *Clark County Park District.* Accessed May 27, 2016. http://www.clarkcountyparks.org/our-parks -trails/leadingham-prairie/.

Conover, Charlotte Reeve. *Dayton, Ohio: An Intimate History.* New York: Lewis Historical Publishing, 1932.

Cooke, James J. *Billy Mitchell.* Boulder, Colorado: Lynne Rienner, 2002.

"Cooperative Agreement between the Department of Defense (DoD) and The Nature Conservancy (TNC)." December 13, 1988, available online at the U.S. Army Corps of Engineers Web site, http://www.usace.army.mil/ Portals/2/docs/civilworks/mous/tnc_mou.pdf.

Crew, Harvey W. *History of Dayton, Ohio.* Dayton: United Brethren Publishing, 1889.

Crouch, Tom D. *The Bishop's Boys: A Life of Wilbur and Orville Wright.* New York: Norton, 1989.

Cusick, Allison W., and K. Roger Troutman. *The Prairie Survey Project: A Summary of Data to Date.* Ohio Biological Survey Informative Circular No. 10. Columbus: Ohio State University, 1978.

Dachnowski, Alfred D. *Peat Deposits of Ohio. Ohio Geological Survey Bulletin* 16 (1912).

Darlington, William M. *An Acccount of the Remarkable Occurences in the Life and Travels of Col. James Smith during His Captivity with the Indians, in the Years 1755, '56, '57, '58, '59.* Cincinnati: Robert Clarke Co., 1907.

———. *Christopher Gist's Journals with Historical, Geographical, and Ethnological Notes, and Biographies of His Contemporaries.* Pittsburgh: J. R. Weldon & Co., 1893.

Davis, Jeffrey G. "Eastern Massasauga at Wright-Patterson Air Force Base in Dayton, Ohio," submitted to WPAFB, 2015. This report may be obtained from the WPAFB Natural Resources Program, 88th Air Base Wing Environmental Branch.

DeVault, Travis L., Bradley F. Blackwell, and Jerrold L. Belant, eds. *Wildlife in Airport Environments: Preventing Animal-Aircraft Collisions through Science-Based Management.* Baltimore: Johns Hopkins University Press, 2013.

Dills, R. S. *History of Greene County Together with Historic Notes on the Northwest and State of Ohio.* Dayton: Odell & Mayer, 1881.

Drury, Augustus Waldo. *History of the City of Dayton and Montgomery County, Ohio.* Vol. 1 of 2. Dayton: S. J. Clarke, 1909.

Dumouchelle, Denise H., and Jeffrey T. de Roche. *Lithologic, Natural-Gamma, Grain Size, and Well-Construction Data for Wright-Patterson Air Force Base, Ohio.* Open-File Report 91–181. Washington, D.C.: U.S. Geological Survey, 1991.

Edgar, John F. 1896. *Pioneer Life in Dayton and Vicinity, 1796–1840.* Dayton: U. B. Publishing House, W. J. Shuey Publisher, 1896.

Forty-Third General Assembly of the State of Ohio. *Acts of a General Nature Passed by the Forty-third State of Ohio.* Columbus: Samuel Medary, State Printer, 1845.

Frederick, Clara May. "A Natural History Study of the Vascular Flora of Cedar Bog, Champaign County, Ohio." *Ohio Journal of Science* 74 (March 1974): 65–116.

Garber, D. W. *Waterwheels and Millstones: A History of Ohio Gristmills and Milling.* Columbus: Ohio Historical Society, 1970.

Garrard, Lewis H. *Memoir of Charlotte Chambers.* Philadelphia: T. K. & P. G. Collins, 1868.

Goldthwait, Richard P. "Scenes in Ohio during the Last Ice Age." Address of the president of the Ohio Academy of Science delivered at the Sixty-Eighth Annual Meeting at Capital University, Bexley, Ohio, April 17, 1959. Reprinted in *Ohio Journal of Science* 111, nos. 2–5 (2013): 7.

Gordon, Robert B. *The Natural Vegetation of Ohio in Pioneer Days.* Columbus: Ohio State University Press, 1969.

Gough, Michael, *The Pulitzer Air Races, American Aviation, and Speed Supremacy, 1920–1925,* Jefferson, North Carolina: McFarland, 2013.

Haas, Jennifer R., Michael F. Kolb, and John D. Richards, *Archaeology, Geomorphology, and Land Use History at Wright-Patterson Air Force Base.* Milwaukee: Great Lakes Archaeological Research Center, 1996.

Hansen, Michael C. "The Ice Age in Ohio." Columbus: *Ohio Department of Natural Resources Division of Geological Survey,* 2008. https://geosurvey.ohio dnr.gov/portals/geosurvey/PDFs/Education/el07.pdf.

———, comp. "The Teays River." *Ohio Department of Natural Resources, Division of Geological Survey GeoFacts, No. 10.* November 1995. https://geo survey.ohiodnr.gov/portals/geosurvey/PDFs/GeoFacts/geof10.pdf.

History Office, Wright-Patterson Air Force Base. *Home Field Advantage: A Century of Partnership between Wright-Patterson Air Force Base and Dayton, Ohio, in the Pursuit of Aeronautical Excellence.* Washington, D.C.: U.S. Superintendent of Documents, 2004.

"Huffman Prairie Flying Field." *eBird: An Online Database of Bird Distribution and Abundance.* Accessed June 10, 2017. http://ebird.org/ebird/hotspot/L2132447?yr=all&m=&rank=mrec.

Hunter, W. H., comp. "Pathfinders of Jefferson County." In *Ohio Archaeological and Historical Publications* 6 (1900): 95–313.

Jacobs, A. M. "Will She Fly?" *Popular Mechanics,* Mar. 1929, 379–85.

Jones, Stephen R., and Ruth Carol Cushman. *The North American Prairie: A Field Guide to the Plants, Wildlife, and Natural History of the Prairie Including Where to Hike and Camp.* Boston: Houghton Mifflin, 2004.

Klippart, John H. *The Principles and Practice of Land Drainage: A Brief History of Underdraining. . . .* Cincinnati: Robert Clarke & Co., 1861.

Knepper, George W. *The Ohio Lands Book.* Columbus: Ohio Auditor of State, 2002.

Knoop, Paul "Nature Comes to Base on a Wing and a Prairie." *Dayton Daily News,* July 25, 1985.

Kost, Michael A., Dennis A. Albert, Joshua G. Cohen, Bradford S. Slaughter, and Rebecca K. Schillo. *Natural Communities of Michigan: Classification and Description, Michigan Natural Features Inventory,* Report Number 2007–21. Lansing: Michigan Department of Natural Resources Wildlife Division and Forest, Mineral and Fire Management Division, 2007.

Lafferty, Michael B. *Ohio's Natural Heritage.* Columbus: Ohio Academy of Science, 1979.

Lepper, Bradley Thomas. *Ohio Archaeology: An Illustrated Chronicle of Ohio's Ancient American Indian Cultures.* Wilmington, Ohio: Orange Frazer Press, 2005.

Map of Greene County, Ohio. Philadelphia: Anthony Byles, 1855.

McCormac, James S., and Gregory Kennedy. 2004. *Birds of Ohio.* Auburn, Washington: Lone Pine, 2004.

McCormac, Jim, and Gary Meszaros. *Wild Ohio: The Best of Our Natural Heritage.* Kent, Ohio: Kent State University Press, 2009.

McEnaney, Marla, Elizabeth Fraterrigo, H. Eliot Foulds, and Thomas Richter. *From Pasture to Runway: Huffman Prairie Flying Field, Wright-Patterson Air Force Base, Cultural Landscape Report, Landscape Implementation Plan, Interpretation Plan.* Washington, D.C.: U.S. Department of the Interior, 2002, available online at the National Park Service Web site, https://www.nps.gov/daav/getinvolved/upload/HPFF-CLR.pdf.

Meiners, Scott J., and David L. Gorchov. "The Soil Seed Pool of Huffman Prairie, a Degraded Ohio Prairie, and Its Potential in Restoration." *Ohio Journal of Science* 94, no. 4 (1994): 82–86.

Metzler, Eric H., and David Adamski. "A New Species of Gnorimoschema Busck, 1900 (*Lepidoptera: Gelechiidae, Gelechiinae*) from Ohio and Ilinois." *Fabreries* 27, no. 1 (2002): 59–68.

Metzler, Eric H., and Roger A. Zebold. "Brief Note: Twenty-Eight Species of Moths New to Ohio from Huffman Prairie, Greene County," *Ohio Journal of Science* 95 (June 1995): 240–42.

———. "Huffman Prairie Inventory of Lepidoptera, June through December 1992, Prepared for The Nature Conservancy, Ohio Chapter, and Wright-Patterson Air Force Base, December 31, 1992." Copy can be obtained from WPAFB Natural Resources Program, 88th Air Base Wing Environmental Branch.

Miami Conservancy District. "Paying for the Flood Prevention Project." *Miami Conservancy District Bulletin* 3, nos. 11 and 12 (1951): 256–57.

Minney, David. "Huffman Prairie: Plant Community Monitoring Report 2014." Submitted to Five Rivers MetroParks. Copy can be obtained from WPAFB Natural Resources Program, 88th Air Base Wing Environmental Branch.

———. "Huffman Prairie Baseline Data." Submitted to Wright-Patterson Air Force Base by Ohio Chapter of The Nature Conservancy, 1990. Copy can be obtained from WPAFB Natural Resources Program, 88th Air Base Wing Environmental Branch.

———. "Huffman Prairie Breeding Bird Census: 2014, Report by Dave Minney for Dave Nolin, Director of Conservation, Five Rivers MetroParks." September 2014. Copy can be obtained from WPAFB Natural Resources Program, 88th Air Base Wing Environmental Branch.

———. "Management and Breeding Birds on a Tallgrass Prairie Remnant, 1990–1993; Huffman Prairie, Ohio." Internal document, Columbus: Ohio Chapter of The Nature Conservancy, 1993.

Moeller, Robert. 1973. "Methods of Prairie Development Used at the Aullwood Audubon Center, Dayton, Ohio." *Ohio Journal of Science* 73, no. 5 (1973): 307–11.

Morgan, Arthur E. *The Miami Conservancy District.* New York: McGraw-Hill, 1951.

Morse, Larry. "John W. Van Cleve, Pioneer Ohio Botanist." Summary of presentation made to the Ohio Academy of Science, April 21, 1967. Copy in possession of David Nolin.

Nationwide Environmental Tile Research. "Wright-Patterson Air Force Base Superfund National Priorities List (NPL) Site." *NETR Online.* October 4, 1989. http://environment.netronline.com/site.php?cid=OH7571724312.

Nolan, John. "C-5 Cargo Planes to Be Replaced by C-17's." *Dayton Daily News,* March 12, 2010.

Nolin, David, and James Runkle. "Prairies and Fens of Bath Township, Greene County, Ohio." *Ohio Journal of Science* 85, no. 3 (1985): 125–30.

Norris, Stanley E., William P. Cross, and Richard P. Goldthwait. *The Water Resources of Greene County, Ohio.* Bulletin no. 19. Columbus: Ohio Department of Natural Resources, Division of Water, 1956.

Ohio Chapter of The Nature Conservancy, *Huffman Prairie Management Plan, Prepared for Wright-Patterson Air Force Base by The Nature Conservancy, Ohio Chapter, March 23 1994,* 2–3, in possession of David Nolin.

———. "Ron and Liz Cramer Receive Award," *Volunteers! Newsletter,* Spring 1995.

———. *Huffman Prairie Management Plan. Prepared for Wright-Patterson Air Force Base by The Nature Conservancy, Ohio Chapter, March 23, 1994.* Columbus: Ohio Chapter of The Nature Conservancy, 1994.

Ohio Department of Natural Resources. "Milford Center Prairie State Natural Area." *Division of Natural Areas and Preserves.* Accessed May 27, 2016. http://naturepreserves.ohiodnr.gov/state-nature-preserves/find-a-state-nature-preserve/milford-center-prairie.

Ohio Department of Natural Resources Division of Widlife. *Bees and Wasps of Ohio.* Publication 5488 (0316). Columbus: Ohio Division of Wildlife, 2016.

———. "Massasauga—*Sistrurus catenatus catenatus.*" Accessed June 10, 2017, *ODNR Division of Wildlife/Species and Habitats/Species Guide Index/Reptiles.* http://wildlife.ohiodnr.gov/species-and-habitats/species-guide-index/reptiles/massasauga.

———."Smooth Greensnake—*Opheodrys vernalis.*" *ODNR Division of Wildlife/Species and Habitats/Species Guide Index/Reptiles.* Accessed June 10, 2017. http://wildlife.ohiodnr.gov/species-and-habitats/species-guide-index/reptiles/smooth-greensnake.

Ohio History Connection. "Turnpikes." In *Ohio History Central.* Accessed February 17, 2016. http://www.ohiohistorycentral.org/w/Turnpikes.

Ohio Invasive Plants Council. "Smooth Brome." *Invasive Plants of Ohio, Fact Sheet 13,* Accessed May 27, 2016. http://www.oipc.info/uploads/5/8/6/5 /5865248I/13factsheetsmoothbrome.pdf.

Ohio Prairie Association. "Claridon Prairie." *Ohio Prairie Association.* Accessed June 21, 2016. http://www.ohioprairie.org/page83.html.

———. "New Latin and Common Names for Ohio Prairie Plant Species." Ohio Prairie Association Web site, accessed April 26, 2016, http://www.ohio prairie.org/pageIIo.html.

Pickard, Bill. "Israel Ludlow: The Man That Surveyed Ohio." *Archaeology Blog.* November 10, 2009. https://www.ohiohistory.org/learn/collections/archae ology/archaeology-blog/2009/november-2009/israel-ludlow-the-man-that -surveyed-ohio.

Pringle, Heather. "The First Americans." *Scientific American,* November 2011, 36–45.

"Reaches for Cucumber—Uncovers Rattlesnake." *Skywrighter,* August 26, 1960.

Renstrom, Arthur George. *Wilbur and Orville Wright: A Reissue of A Chronology Commemorating the Hundredth Anniversary of the Birth of Orville Wright, August 19, 1871.* Washington, D.C.: National Aeronautics and Space Administration, Office of External Relations, 2003.

Richard, Benjamin H., Richard J. Kulibert, Paul J. Wolfe, and Benjamin Hudson. *Delineation of the Ancestral Drainage Paths of the Mad River, near Dayton, Ohio.* Technical report series. Dayton: Wright State University Department of Geology, 1979.

Riddell, John Leonard. "A Synopsis of the Flora of the Western States," *Western Journal of the Medical and Physical Sciences* 8 (1835): 489–566. Republished as *A Synopsis of the Flora of the Western States.* Cincinnati: E. Deming, 1835.

Riddell, Levi, and W. D. Riddell. *Riddell's Atlas of Greene County.* Xenia, Ohio: Levi and W. D. Riddell, 1896.

Roach, Edward J. *The Wright Company: From Invention to Industry.* Athens: Ohio University Press, 2013.

Robinson, George F. *History of Greene County, Ohio: Embracing the Organization of the County. . . .* Xenia, Ohio: S. J. Clark, 1902.

Rodewald, Paul G., Matthew B. Shumar, Aaron T. Boone, David L. Slager, and Jim McCormac, eds. *The Second Atlas of Breeding Birds in Ohio.* University Park: Pennsylvania State University Press, 2016.

Schramm, Peter, David S. Schramm, and Stephen G. Johnson. "Seasonal Phenology and Habitat Selection of the Sedge Wren Cistothorus platensis, in a Restored Tallgrass Prairie." *The Prairie: Past, Present, and Future: Proceedings of the Ninth North American Prairie Conference, Held July 29–August 1, 1984, Moorhead, Minnesota.* Edited by Gary K. Clambey and Richard H. Pemble. Fargo: Tri-College University Center for Environmental Studies, North Dakota State University, 1986.

Schumacher, Gregory A., Michael P. Angle, Brian E. Mott, and Douglass J. Aden. "Geology of the Dayton Region in Core and Outcrop: A Workshop and Field Trip for Citizens, Environmental Investigators, Geologists, and Educators." Ohio Department of Natural Resources, Division of Geological

Survey Open-File Report, 2012. Available online at Ohio Department of Natural Resources Web site,https://geosurvey.ohiodnr.gov/portals/geo survey/PDFs/OpenFileReports/OFR_2012–1.pdf.

Sharp, Harold S. *The Courtmartial of Billy Mitchell*. Metuchen, New Jersey: Scarecrow, 1977.

Steele, Robert Wilbur, and Mary Davies Steele. *Early Dayton*. Dayton: U. B. Publishing House, W. J. Shuey Publisher, 1896.

Stewart, Omer C. *Forgotten Fires: Native Americans and the Transient Wilderness*. Edited by Henry T. Anderson and Kat Lewis. Norman: University of Oklahoma Press, 2002.

Stuckey, Ronald L., and Guy L. Denny. "Prairie Fens and Bog Fens in Ohio: Floristic Similarities, Differences, and Geographical Affinities." In *Geobotany II*. Edited by R. C. Romans, 1–33. New York: Plenum, 1981.

Stuckey, Ronald L., and James S. Pringle. "Type Localities of Vascular Plants First Described from Ohio." *SIDA Contributions to Botany* 20, no. 4 (2003): 1687.

Stuckey, Ronald L., and Karen J. Reese, eds. *The Prairie Peninsula—In the "Shadow" of Transeau: Proceedings of the Sixth North American Prairie Conference, the Ohio State University Columbus, Ohio 12–17 August 1978*. Columbus: College of Biological Sciences, Ohio State University, 1981.

Sugg, Zachary. "Assessing U.S. Farm Drainage: Can GIS Lead to Better Estimates of Subsurface Drainage Extent?" *World Resources Institute*. August 2007. http://www.wri.org/publication/assessing-us-farm-drainage.

Swan, J. R. *Revised Statutes of the State of Ohio, of a General Nature*. Cincinnati: R. Clarke & Co., 1870.

Teetor, H. B. 1885. *Life and Times of Israel Ludlow*. Cincinnati: Cranston & Stowe, 1885.

U.S. Census Bureau, Schedule 4, Production of Agriculture in Bath Township in the County of Greene in the Post Office Osborn, 1860, 29.

U.S. Department of Agriculture, Natural Resources Conservation Service Plants Database. Accessed April 26, 2017, https://plants.usda.gov/.

U.S. Department of the Interior, Bureau of Land Management. *General Land Office Records*. Accessed February 17, 2016, http://www.glorecords.blm.gov/.

U.S. Fish and Wildlife Service. "Eastern Massasauga (*Sistrurus catenatus*) Status: Proposed at Threatened." *U.S. Fish and Wildlife Service Endangered Species*. Accessed May 27, 2016. http://www.fws.gov/midwest/endangered /reptiles/eama/.

———. "Indiana Bat (Myotis sodalis) Fact Sheet." *Endangered Species*. Last updated July 19, 2016. http://www.fws.gov/midwest/endangered/mammals/inba/inbafctsht.html.

Vischer, Peter. "When Men Race with Death to Make the Air Safe." *Popular Science Monthly*, January 1925, 36, 37, 144.

Walker, Lois E., and Shelby E. Wickam. *From Huffman Prairie to the Moon: The History of Wright-Patterson Air Force Base*. [Dayton:] WPAFB Office of History, 2750th Air Base Wing, 1986.

Walton, William C., and George D. Scudder. *Ground Water Resources of the Valley Train Deposits in the Fairborn Area, Technical Report #3*. Columbus: Ohio Division of Natural Resources, Division of Water, 1960.

Weaver, John E. *Prairie Plants and Their Environment*. Lincoln: University of Nebraska Press, 1968.

White, Albert C. *A History of the Rectangular Survey System.* Washington, D.C.: U.S. Department of the Interior, Bureau of Land Management, 1983.

Williams, James L. *Blazes, Posts, and Stones: A History of Ohio's Original Land Subdivisions.* Akron: University of Akron Press, 2015.

Woods, Alan J., James M. Omernik, C. Scott Brockman, Timothy D. Gerber, William D. Hosteter, and Sandra H. Azevedo. *Ecoregions of Indiana and Ohio.* Reston, Virginia: U.S. Dept. of the Interior, U.S. Geological Survey, 1998.

Wright-Patterson Air Force Base. "Environmental Assessment to Implement the Integrated Natural Resources Management Plan, Wright-Patterson Air Force Base, Ohio, 88th Civil Engineer Group, September 2016." http://www .wpafb.af.mil/Portals/60/documents/Index/environmental/160913-Environ mental-Natural-resources-management-plan.pdf?ver=2016–09–13–140613 –413

Young, Roz. "Bicycle Enthusiasm Sparked Friendship with the Wrights." *Dayton Daily News,* September 6, 1997.

Index